AMEN ALL BY MYSELF!

AMEN ALL BY MYSELF!

DISCOVERING GOD IN LIFE'S WILDERNESS

SHERWOOD CARTHEN
WITH PHIL AND LINDA SOMMERVILLE

Amen, All By Myself

ISBN 978-0-615-28084-4

Cover Design by Dave Eaton
Cover Photo of Sherwood Carthen by Darren Takegami

Printed in the United States of America

To the love of my life – Charlene, my wife.

Your constant love, devotion, and tug have won out and we now have some of our story to share with many others.

CONTENTS

Acknowledgements

The stories in this book were born out of a community of faith that was willing to follow God's call into unknown territory. I am so thankful for the incredible people of the Family Worship Center who walked through this amazing journey with me. God used you to help shape who I am today and I am forever grateful.

It was also a true joy to minister for over twenty years at FWC alongside my sister, Regina, and the rest of my family. Your partnership in the Gospel helped set the stage for what only God could do and encouraged me to pursue God's call to diversity and authentic relationships. I thank God for each of you.

To my friends Chuck O'Neil, and Ray and Kim Myers, I thank you for your commitment and dedication to see this project through. Your willingness to sacrifice proves your love for God, His Kingdom, and me. Thanks for believing in the unseen.

My heartfelt thanks go to my writers, Phil and Linda Sommerville. Your work on this project is unmatched. The willingness to put your own needs on hold and give full attention to the book will always amaze me. Your insight and ability to hear the story only once and then turn those thoughts and ideas into script was more than brilliant. Your wisdom to pursue the dream and your faithfulness to see it through has made us partners for life. Thank you for your undying love. Without you this would not have been possible.

To Ray Johnston, thank you for your great friendship, amazing vision, incredible faith and especially thank you for giving me the opportunity to live a dream. God used my wilderness experience to prepare me for the day our paths would cross and my life would be changed forever. God has richly blessed me through your friendship.

I also need to give a special "shout out" to BOSS (Bayside of South Sacramento), my current church family. You are a dream come true. Thank you for allowing me the privilege of being your pastor and seeing a bit of heaven unfold here on earth.

Above all, I give thanks to Jesus Christ, my Savior and Lord. You are the Author of my life and the true Author of this book. I love you and will continue to follow You anywhere—even into the wilderness.

Sherwood Carthen

Foreword

Every Christian I know is looking for what this book provides—HOPE! Intensely personal, deeply moving and spiritually challenging, *Amen All By Myself* is relentlessly inspiring. Just like my friend Sherwood Carthen.

Our friendship began a few years ago with a simple introduction. A growing admiration has deepened the relationship. Simply put – I don't know anyone else like him.

Five years ago, in his own words, he was in the wilderness, wondering if God had put him on the shelf.

Today…

- Sherwood is pastoring Bayside of South Sacramento, one of the fastest-growing churches in the nation.
- His commitment to justice is making his church a model for multi-cultural churches.
- His "Bless A Family" Christmas event brings Christmas to more kids than any other event in the state capital.
- His relational ability is bringing the Christian community in Sacramento together like no one else.

None of this looked possible in the recent past. And what makes this book so valuable is that, writing from personal experience, Sherwood demonstrates that tough times need not stop God from doing great things in your future!

If you, like Sherwood, find yourself needing the power...to start over; to hang in there; to overcome a crippling habit; to come back after a failed marriage; to bounce back from a heart-breaking loss; to let go of guilt and live with integrity; to believe that it is never too late to become the person God wanted you to become in the first place—you have picked up the right book.

Our nation, its people and particularly its leaders are crying out for hope. I predict that anyone reading and applying the principles in this book will never recover. This is a spiritual life gold mine. So is Sherwood Carthen!

Ray Johnston
Senior Pastor, Bayside of Granite Bay, CA

Introduction

In the year 2000, something miraculous happened—my predominantly black church in the city merged with a predominantly white church in the suburbs. Then all hell broke loose in my life.

I knew God was doing a powerful work in the church. What I didn't know was how powerful His work would be in my own life. After surrendering my church to God, He led me straight into the wilderness. It was the last place I wanted—or expected—to go. But it became clear that if I wanted to follow God, I had to go through a desert of testing.

I should not have been surprised. After all, Jesus himself had to go through the wilderness before being released into His public ministry. And even though you won't hear this in many places, you need to know that God will lead you into the wilderness at some point as well.

This journey is not for the faint of heart—it's for those who are ready for more of God. I speak from experience. I've been to the wilderness and it's tough—but necessary.

God takes us there because it's the place where we see Him most clearly. It's the place where His life takes root in us most deeply. And it's the place where the desert heat burns away the junk in our lives so we're ready for the new work God has planned for us.

The good news is that the wilderness is not some random event happening in our lives. It's not a result of the devil grabbing the steering wheel of our lives and taking control. God is at work and He has a purpose for each of us in the wilderness. And if God is behind our wilderness experience, we need to cooperate with Him, not resist Him. We need to pass the test so we'll have a testimony. We need to allow God to turn our scars into stars.

So allow me to serve as your wilderness guide. Let me help you uncover the meaning in your struggle and point out the incredible things God is doing in your life. As you read on, know that God has placed this book in your hands at this particular moment because He loves you, and has a purpose for you. You're not alone on this wilderness journey. God and I will be right here encouraging you along the way.

Chapter One

Stuck on the Bench

"'For I know the plans I have for you,' declares the LORD, 'plans to prosper you and not to harm you, plans to give you hope and a future.'"
Jeremiah 29:11

"I've been a starter my whole life," he grumbled, "so why am I sitting on the bench?" Hurt and anger flashed in his eyes, but I had no easy answer for him. I just listened as he gained steam and exploded, "I've started all through high school and college, and my entire NBA career. I started every game of the NBA Finals. But now, I'm sitting on the bench and I don't know why!"

As chaplain for the Sacramento Kings, I've walked through many tough times with players. On this particular night, Nick Anderson was in a bad place. Nick was a former first-round draft choice and a proven veteran, but in his second season with the Kings not only was he not starting, he wasn't even playing.

Frustrated

As I listened to Nick, I understood his frustration. For the past year I'd felt like God—*my* coach—had taken me out of the game and put me on the bench, and I didn't know why. We were both frustrated. He was frustrated with his coach, and I was frustrated with God.

God—my coach—had taken me out of the game and put me on the bench, and I didn't know why.

I wondered why God had led me to merge my predominantly black church with a predominantly white church and then taken me out of ministry. I wondered why God had given me the gifts and calling of a pastor only to tell me to sit down and be quiet. I even wondered if God was through with me. Was this the end of my story?

Nick and I were both experiencing dry times in our lives. We were both in a place that the Bible often refers to as a wilderness. Nick had been benched from the game, and I had been "benched" from preaching. We were both struggling to make sense of our situations, and we both needed to make a choice.

In Danger

As Nick talked with me that night I realized that he was in danger—more danger than he knew. There was more at stake than playing time. There was even more at stake than his career. With every game spent on the bench, I could see Nick's attitude plummet. His very character was on the line, and how he chose to respond to this dry time would determine who he was as a man and who he would be in the future.

Then it hit me—God was using Nick to show me that I was in

danger as well. There was more at stake than my ministry career. Who I was and who I would be in the future, in fact, my very character, would be determined by how I responded to God in this wilderness time.

For Grown Folks

In my church, when we talk about serious things we say, "This is for grown folks." That's what this book is—a book for grown folks, because talking about the wilderness is tough.

Everybody goes through wilderness times. Things go wrong and you don't know why. Sometimes it's a tragedy that puts you in a bad place, or it's a crisis, or a bad decision. Other times, as far as you know, you did everything right. Your motives were pure, your actions were selfless, your decisions seemed to have been led by God—yet you're struggling. Your money has run out, your health has failed, people are standing against you, or all these things and worse are happening to you.

When you experience these times it can feel like your life no longer counts for anything. Things just don't make sense. You begin to despair. Your attitude plummets. And you're in danger—more danger than you know.

God Is Not Finished With You

Have you ever been there? Are you there right now? If not, I guarantee you will be at some point. But before you get discouraged and close this book, listen up. I'm writing this book for you. God is not finished with you yet. He has a purpose for you in this wilderness.

You may not see what God's up to yet. As you start this book, you might not be sharing my excitement about what can happen in the wilderness. For right now, I might have to say, "Amen, all by myself," but don't give up on me. I want to help you see that this wilderness is a good thing and that God is using it to do a good work in your life. When you discover God's purpose for you in this dry place, you'll choose to say "amen" too. You'll be able to embrace all that He has for you, and you'll come to know that He is a good God who has good plans for you.

You're Not Alone

Has it ever occurred to you that there isn't a major player in the Bible who didn't go through a wilderness time? Noah, Abraham, Joseph, Moses, Naomi, David, Jonah (actually, Jonah went through a wet time), Mary, Jesus—you name the major players, and they went through hard times. It's important to realize that they didn't go through these wilderness experiences *in spite of* being great. No, the truth is that before they could do great things, they had to learn God's wilderness lessons.

God taught me some life-changing lessons in the wilderness—lessons I needed to learn before He could do great things in my life. God wants to do great things in your life, too. But first there are lessons God must teach you.

It's Your Choice

You have a choice to make. You need to decide how you will respond when you find yourself in the wilderness. Will you embrace the experience, or will you take a short cut and run away? Will you learn the lessons God has for you, or will you miss out? God is waiting for you in the wilderness, and He wants to know—will you follow Him? Your decision will determine who you are and who you will become.

For one NBA player, on one specific night, God had me in the right place at the right time. I was able to help Nick that night because I was experiencing the same thing myself. I knew exactly what he was going through. So after listening to his frustrations, I told him what I'm about to tell you. I said, "Nick, let me tell you a story…"

Chapter Two

They Thought I Was Crazy

"Many are the plans in a man's heart,

but it is the LORD'S purpose that prevails."

Proverbs 19:21

I was the king of a kingdom. I don't mean to sound arrogant, but the reality is that when you're the pastor of a black church, you're a king. In our country, there's supposed to be a separation of church and state—but in the black community, the church *is* the state.

If community leaders and politicians want to meet with the people, they meet in your church. If the neighborhood wants to rally or complain about the city, they meet in your church. On Sunday mornings, people come to church to get their marching orders for how to live. A black pastor can endorse a candidate or a proposition without ever using the word "endorse." But people understand what you're doing and they will follow.

Our church in South Sacramento was an important part of the community. We were on the radio and television. We ran multiple community-based programs that met the needs of our neighbors. We were making a real difference.

I had influence—I knew the mayor, the chief of police, city council members, the movers and shakers in our city. It seemed like God had set me up for success—like things were really going to happen. My ministry was "on and crackin," as I like to say.

I was the pastor of a black church—the king of a kingdom, the head of state. But I gave it all up.

Red & Yellow, Black & White – Except in the Church

When I started pastoring, I was bi-vocational. Monday through Friday, I worked with people of all colors and races at the Department of Motor Vehicles. My office was diverse. The classes at Sacramento City College where I went to school were diverse. The stores where I shopped were diverse. Everywhere I went there was diversity. However, on Sundays at my church, nearly everyone was black. This made no sense to me, but what could be done about it? I had no clue. But God did.

God's first move was to pull the rug out from under our church. We lost the lease on our facilities, and we had to find a new place to meet. So I brought our leadership together and said, "Look folks, we knew God wanted us in this facility so we could expand our ministry. We didn't think it could be done, but God made it happen. Now God is moving us again, and we need to make sure that the next place we go is the place where God leads us. We need to make sure that the way we feel about the next place is the way we felt when we moved here."

Over the next several months, we toured several possible facilities. However, each time we gathered to pray, we sensed that God was saying, "No. This isn't the place I have for you."

We couldn't figure it out. These buildings were all within our community. They all had ample space. We could keep our ministry going and even growing. We had the money to make it happen. But we didn't sense God's confirmation.

How would that look if all the white people left the building and then all the black people came in?

That's when I had a dream: I dreamt I was worshiping in a church, and when I looked around, there weren't just black folks worshiping there. I saw people of different ethnicities and colors—I saw diversity. Then I noticed that the preacher in my dream was the pastor of Harvest Church—a white church in the suburbs, ten miles from our church.

Doin' Something Crazy

I pulled our leadership together and told them about the dream. I explained that we needed to pray because I didn't know if this dream was from God. As we prayed, we began sensing that this dream may be the Spirit's leading. So I did something crazy. I gave the pastor of Harvest Church a call.

Over the phone, I explained to the pastor our need for a place to meet while we looked for a more permanent location. I told him that we believed God wanted us to worship at his church.

The pastor was gracious and said he would love to have us. He told me that their services were over by 12:30 p.m. and we could come in and have our service after that. He misunderstood me.

"No," I replied. "How would that look if all the white people left the building and then all the black people came in? What I'm talking about is having our congregation worship *with* your congregation in the same service." There was a long moment of silence before he spoke again.

To his credit he didn't say, "No." He said, "We'll need to pray about that." Over the next few weeks, we prayed and God confirmed to all of us that this was the path to take. We worked out the details and soon our black city church was worshiping with a white suburban church. It was only meant to be a 90-day arrangement while we looked for new facilities.

While the leadership of our church was supportive, I can't say that my congregation was jumping up and down with excitement. They went along because they trusted me. They knew we needed a place to meet. Besides, it was only going to be temporary. God just chuckled.

Becoming One

Then I had another dream: I heard the Spirit of the Lord say, "You cannot leave the same way you came in." I knew God was referring to the way our churches were operating.

Although we were worshiping together, we were operating as two completely separate churches. We went so far as to have separate sets of announcements and separate offerings all within the same service. It was a mess. It was "us and them."

Now, I sensed the Spirit of the Lord telling me that the only thing that would please Him was if our two churches became one.

I took the dream seriously.

I met with the pastor of Harvest Church and shared my dream. I also pulled my leaders together and said, "We've got to pray about this." Not only did we need to seek God about merging our churches but also about coming under the leadership of the white church. I knew that if God led us to join that larger white church, I couldn't be part of their pastoral staff. I would have to step down and join the congregation; otherwise it would appear that we merged so that I could obtain a bigger "kingdom," and that would undermine everything I believed God wanted to do.

For the next several weeks, we prayed and studied our Bibles. Then our leaders came together and we voted. The vote was 32-3 in favor of dissolving our church and merging with the white church. And that's what we did.

They Thought I was Crazy

Then came the criticism. Although our church's leadership strongly believed in this move, there were those in our congregation who were not supportive. There were many more in the African-American community who strongly disagreed with what we were doing.

If you're not from the black community, you may not fully grasp the gravity of this situation. You may hear this story and think, *"Isn't that nice that these two churches joined together."* But you have to understand that in the black community, this was serious.

For many within the African-American community, the idea of closing a successful and vibrant church that served the community was dead wrong. And even worse was the fact that we were giving up our church to a *white* church. It seemed like we were subverting our identity to the dominant culture.

People thought I was crazy. They thought I had literally lost my mind. I was giving up my kingdom. I was giving up a successful ministry. I was giving up my influence and my very identity. And my church was giving up these things as well.

After the merge, there was a time of real shake-up; a number of white folks left to go to other white churches and a number of our folks left to go to other black churches. However, those who remained were excited about what God was doing. We sensed we were doing the right thing. We sensed the Spirit was leading.

A Story of Racial Healing

It wasn't long before God confirmed to me that we were doing the right thing. He set up a "divine appointment" with Lois Margaret Alston, a dignified, 80-year-old woman from our church who told me a powerful story.

She explained how God led her, along with her daughter, back to church after years of not attending. "When we started coming a few years ago," she said, "I told God that you were going to be my pastor from now on. But then you shared this idea of merging our church with a white church, and I'll tell you upfront—I thought you were crazy."

"Oh great," I thought. *"Here comes more criticism."* But I was in for a surprise.

"I want to tell you *why* I thought you were crazy," she continued, "and what God has done as a result." Lois proceeded to share her story—a story filled with injustice and pain—and I was overcome with emotion.

Way back in 1937, she and her brother had been valedictorians of their high school class in Kansas City. However, because they were black, they weren't allowed to speak at the commencement. Instead, a white person was chosen for that honor. Lois was hurt and bitter from this experience and from that point on she vowed to have nothing to do with white people.

"But then," she said pointing her finger at me, "you said we were going to merge with this *white* church and that this *white* man was going to be my pastor. I wanted to walk away right then." She paused and smiled. "But I didn't."

Instead, Lois allowed God to heal her heart. God used this merger to bring healing and freedom to her life. In fact, she was so free that she was able to shake the hand of our new white pastor, look him in the eye and tell him, "You are my pastor now."

Seven months later, Lois died and went to be with the Lord. For more than 60 years she walked around nursing a wounded heart and carrying a grudge, but she died with her heart reconciled and the animosity removed. God had done a powerful healing in her. I felt that if this was the only good thing to ever come from the merger, it would all have been worth it—but there were many other blessings still to come.

For the first time, whites could invite their black friends to church without being afraid that they would feel out of place. Blacks could invite their white friends without worrying they would feel uncomfortable. Then something really interesting began to happen: people from all races started to hear about a church that looked a little bit like heaven—and they started to come. God was pleased, and the church exploded.

What's Next, God?

After seeing God do this great work, I waited for His next call for me in ministry. I was sure it would come soon because I had been a faithful servant and had accomplished the task God set before me. I couldn't wait to see what great thing God was going to call me to do next. But the call didn't come.

People from all races started to hear about a church that looked a little bit like heaven—and they started to come.

At the very least, I thought, God would have me guest preach while I waited for the next big thing to happen. After all, God had called me to be a preacher. Besides, I was well known in the city, and I was well connected with pastors in both black and white churches. I was also the bishop of an association of independent churches in our area. I was certain I would soon be receiving invitations to preach. But the phone didn't ring.

This was not what I expected. I had done everything right. How could this be happening? And *why* was it happening?

I was in a lonely place. Instead of being on the platform using my gift of preaching, I was sitting on the pew worshiping, just like everyone else. I began to wonder if maybe God had accomplished his purpose for my life. Maybe God was through with me.

I didn't realize it at the time, but God was taking me into the wilderness.

Four Promises

During this time of confusion, I cried out to God in desperation, asking for some guidance. I needed answers. During prayer one day, I sensed God impress four promises upon me. God promised me that:

1) I would pastor again.
2) It would be to the masses.
3) It would be in a multi-cultural context.
4) It would be with a non-traditional partner.

Now those first three things made sense to me. I could picture in my mind how they might happen. However, the fourth thing really confused me.

Even though I didn't understand it all, the message was so clear that I immediately wrote it down. Yet I had to wonder—did I actually hear from God or had I just written down some wishful thoughts?

A few days later, I received a phone call that literally knocked me over. Mother Davis, an older member of our church, called and began boldly speaking to me. This saint had been a mighty woman of prayer for decades and her spiritual sensitivity was acute. I barely said, "Hello," before she launched in.

"Pastor," she said, "I just finished praying and God showed me things." Then she started telling me about all the things people were saying about me. It was like she had been reading my mail. She couldn't have known some of these things unless God had revealed them to her. Tears filled my eyes, but the bombshell was yet to come.

"Pastor," she went on without taking a breath, "God told me something about you. God told me that you would pastor again and it would be in my lifetime. Not only are you gonna pastor, but it will be to the masses. And it will be to every race and color. And" —I could not believe I was hearing this—"it will be with a non-traditional partner." I literally fell to the floor.

My wife, Charlene, came rushing in, wondering what terrible thing had happened. She thought maybe somebody had died. All I could do was hold her and weep. I couldn't even speak.

There was no way Mother Davis could have known about the four promises God had given me, but through this incredible saint, God confirmed His message to me. I didn't know what it all meant, but I knew God was not through with me. I was humbled and overjoyed.

But as I found out later, I had a long wilderness journey ahead of me before these promises came true.

Still Stuck On The Bench

It was a full year later that Nick Anderson poured out his frustrations to me right before a Sacramento Kings game. I understood how he felt. Even though God had given me promises of what He would do in my life, nothing was happening. While Nick was struggling on the bench, I was stuck on the bench myself.

I had lost my identity as "pastor." I was no longer "the preachin' machine." I was sitting on the pew listening to someone else preach. I felt isolated. There were people who thought I'd lost my mind. I had no income. The phone wasn't ringing, and I was in the wilderness.

As I sat there with Nick moments before the game, I knew God had put me there that night just for him. Nick felt isolated—I felt isolated, too. He was frustrated because he wasn't doing what he was gifted for—I was frustrated, too. He felt he was losing his identity because he wasn't getting any playing time—I felt that way, too.

So after sharing my story, I looked him in the eye and said, "Nick, God hasn't forgotten you. In fact, He's got you on the bench because He's dealing with you. God is taking you through the wilderness because He loves you, man."

Nick could see that I knew what I was talking about, and in that moment Nick made an important choice. He chose to embrace what God was doing in his life. He realized he didn't have to play basketball to have value. In fact, Nick decided that what God wanted most from him during that dry time was to change his attitude and become the best team member he could be. And that's exactly what he did.

That night Nick went out and cheered his team on. He stood up, waved towels, showed support, and began to be the man that God made him to be. His attitude changed that night. And as the season went on, he became a new man.

At first, I thought God had me there that night just for Nick, but now I see that God also used Nick to help me. After that night, I realized I needed to embrace my wilderness. I needed to get a new attitude. I needed to become a humble servant that God could really use.

Amen, All By Myself

Now if I were preaching this message in a black church, the congregation would encourage me right about now by saying "amen." But during my time in the wilderness, I found myself saying "amen" all by myself. There weren't many people standing with me or encouraging me during this time. Yet because of the promises God gave me, I was able to stand alone knowing I was right where He wanted me.

The funny thing is that after that night with Nick, I began to think, "Hey, I've finally got this—I've learned what the wilderness has to teach me. God, I'm ready to come out of the wilderness now." God just chuckled.

It would be three more years before God would bring me out of the wilderness and fulfill His promises. And I needed every minute.

Chapter Three

Led By The Spirit

"Then Jesus was led by the Spirit into the desert...."

Matthew 4:1

After merging our churches, I was exhilarated. I couldn't wait to see what God would do next. I was certain that God would use me to do something even bigger and better because I had been obedient, even in the face of criticism.

I couldn't imagine how God was going to top what I had just experienced, but I was sure He would. I was pumped up and ready to take on the world. *"C'mon God,"* I thought, *"what's the next big thing you want me to do? I'm ready for anything!"*

I was wrong. I wasn't at all ready for what God was going to do.

What Just Happened?

I suddenly found myself without a job. Worse, no one was calling me. I had no income and no prospects. It was like I had fallen off the planet. I was the forgotten man. God had swept me aside and moved on without me—as if He no longer needed me. In a blink, I had gone from the mountaintop to the desert.

I didn't get it. I thought that I'd done everything right. I had followed the Spirit. Yet I landed in the wilderness? This wasn't right. What was I doing in the wilderness? I desperately needed to understand what was happening.

The Verse that Rocked My World

Then God led me to read something in the Bible that rocked my world. It was a simple phrase—just a few words. I'd read it countless times before, but had never paid attention to what it really said. If you feel like you're in a wilderness and you're desperate to understand why—PAY ATTENTION. This might rock your world too.

If you feel like you're in a wilderness and you're desperate to understand why—PAY ATTENTION.

Before I share the verse, let me set the scene. Toward the end of Matthew 3, Jesus comes to John the Baptist to be baptized. If you think about it, this doesn't make sense. John had been baptizing people who were repenting of their sins, but Jesus is the mighty Son of God. He had no sins. He should be baptizing John, not submitting to John for baptism. Yet this is what the Father wanted. Jesus could assert His authority here, but he doesn't. He chooses to obey the Father and carry out His will.

When Jesus comes up out of the water, the Father is so pleased that He shouts from heaven saying: "Yes, that's my son! He did it right. I am really pleased with him." It is an exhilarating moment. I can picture Jesus after an experience like that saying, "Father, I did what you told me to do. I'm ready to go. Let's do this!"

But look what happens instead. Matthew 4:1 says, "Then Jesus was led up by the Spirit into the wilderness."

Did you catch that? In an instant, Jesus went from a powerful baptism experience to the desert. He goes from the ultimate mountain top to the darkest valley. Compared to that, my own mountaintop-to-desert experience seems like nothing. But that's not what rocked me. What really rocked my world was the reason why Jesus landed in the desert. The text says that Jesus was led there "*by the Spirit.*"

"What?" I thought. "*You've got to be kidding me! Jesus is in the desert because God* wants *him there? He is taken to the wilderness because of His obedience?"* This blew my mind. I believed that desert experiences were bad things, not rewards for obedience. I thought that if you were in the desert it was a sign that you had been demoted, not promoted; but now those mistaken beliefs were being shattered by the truth that confronted me in this single verse.

I thought I had landed in the wilderness because God had either ignored my obedience or decided I was no longer needed, but now I realized that the opposite was true.

God was actively involved in my life. Just as the Spirit led Jesus to the wilderness, God was intentionally bringing me into the wilderness. My obedience had shown God that I was ready for more, but first God had to prepare me.

Making Sense of your Wilderness

If you find yourself in a wilderness and you're confused as to why, I have good news. *You're there because God has plans for you, but He needs to prepare you for them.* If you don't grasp this truth, you'll never make sense of your wilderness experience.

You must know this: *It's the Spirit who leads you into the wilderness!* Once you understand this, you'll be ready to embrace the wilderness and learn the lessons God wants to teach you. God has plans for you, but before He will trust you with His power, you must learn some wilderness lessons.

This may not sound like good news. In fact, you may wonder why God would "reward" your obedience with hardship, but I've learned that the wilderness is a good thing—hard, but good. My prayer is that this book will become your guide to understanding God's purposes for the wilderness so that when you find yourself there, you won't get lost or feel abandoned.

But I need to keep it real. God's wilderness training school will be difficult. The results, however, will be life-changing. Your ability to trust God will skyrocket and your sensitivity to His leading will mushroom. God will use the hardships of the wilderness to shape you into a powerful tool for His purposes.

If you're ready to learn how to navigate the wilderness, the first thing you must learn is how to be led by the Spirit.

Being Led by the Spirit

I have frequently been asked, "What made you so sure that the Spirit was leading you to merge your church?"

Some people ask me that question because they're skeptics,

while others ask for a more powerful reason. They ask because they desperately want to be led by the Spirit. They want to experience God, not just talk about God. They want to be used by God, not hide from God. They want to get in the game, not sit on the bench.

God does great things through people who are desperate to be led by the Spirit. I want to do all I can to help you be a person who is led by the Spirit, so let me share with you how our church knew we were being led by the Spirit when we decided to merge.

Going to God Empty-Handed

Several years before the merger, our church studied the book *Experiencing God* by Henry Blackaby. When we started the study, there was no way we could have imagined the dramatic ways God was going to use it in our lives. Much of what I've learned about the leading of the Spirit came from the Scriptural lessons learned from that book.

The most important lesson we learned from *Experiencing God* was to go to God empty-handed. This caused us to pray in a new way. Instead of going to God with our own plans and agendas, we learned to come before God without any agenda and ask, "God, what are you doing that you want us to join?" It's a seemingly small shift, but it made an incredible difference.

Once we stopped focusing on our plans, we became available to God's plans—and He surprised us with unexpected opportunities. We were beginning to allow God to take us in directions we could have never dreamed up ourselves. By going to God empty-handed, we gave the Spirit the opportunity to lead us.

Reading with Anticipation

Experiencing God also changed the way we looked at daily Bible study. As we committed ourselves to this practice, something interesting started to happen. We began to notice how Scripture passages we were studying ended up directly applying to unexpected situations that arose.

Through these experiences we began to realize how the Spirit used God's word to lead and prepare us for circumstances that we had no idea were coming. Soon, we were reading Scripture with a sense of anticipation. We wondered how God would use what we read to prepare us for His plans. As a result, the intensity of our personal times with God increased dramatically, and the fruit was evident in the life of our church.

Listening Carefully

We applied these lessons to our personal lives and practiced them in our church life as well. Whenever our church needed to make a decision, the leaders gathered to study the Bible and pray. Then we asked God to show us what He was doing and how He wanted us to join Him. Finally, we asked people to share what they were hearing from God.

These were rich times. Since we were coming before God without an agenda, no one felt pressured to support a certain position. People shared their thoughts openly and everyone listened carefully. When there seemed to be agreement among us, we made our decision and acted on it in faith. With practice, our sensitivity to the leading of the Spirit grew stronger and our decision-making improved.

Ready for a Miracle

Because of the time we spent practicing these lessons, we were ready when God wanted to do a miracle. After I had my dream about merging our church, we did what we had become accustomed to doing. I gathered our leaders for Bible study and prayer. Afterwards, I asked people to share what they were sensing. What happened next left me astounded. It was clear that God was speaking.

One woman, with tears in her eyes, said that over the last few weeks she had been reading in Ephesians 2 that Jesus had "destroyed the barrier, the dividing wall of hostility."

"Now, I know why I was reading that," she said.

"What? You were reading that?" I was stunned. God seemed to have been using her daily Bible study to prepare her for this moment.

Then someone else spoke up. "I've been reading Jesus' command in Matthew 28 that we are to make disciples of all nations. We've been doing a good job of discipling black folks and a few others, but this would really allow us to follow Christ's command."

I couldn't believe what I was hearing. It was amazing how Scripture that people "just happened" to be studying, lined up with the dream I had. Through the living word, God's Spirit was preparing our leaders to make a monumental decision that had not even been on their radar screens.

If I were to describe how we felt the night our church decided to merge, I would use the words spoken in Acts 15:28. These words were originally spoken by the leaders of the Jerusalem church after they'd made their own monumental decision. They sensed God leading them to allow Gentiles into their all-Jewish church, and they explained their decision by saying, "It seemed good to the Holy Spirit and to us." That's exactly how we felt.

Recognizing God's voice only happens when we love God enough to spend time—a lot of time—in His presence.

God called, we followed, and a miracle occurred. A predominately black church in the city merged with a predominately white church in the suburbs. This is what happens when you are led by the Spirit.

You've Got to Put in the Time

My wife, Charlene, is petite, 5'3", and gorgeous. Someone her size could easily hide in a crowd, but not from me. I would recognize her shape, her hair, and her walk from any angle. Her voice would stand out because I know its tone and the way she emphasizes different words. Why do I know these things about my wife? It's because I love her, and I spend a lot time with her. I know her well.

In John 10:4, Jesus says that His people know Him well, too. His "sheep follow Him because they know His voice." The problem is that we live lives that are filled with activities and demands. We live lives that are constantly being bombarded with the noise of people's conflicting opinions. With all that noise, how will we ever recognize God's voice?

Recognizing God's voice only happens when we love God enough to spend time—a lot of time—in His presence. It's only when you spend time with God that His voice becomes distinct.

This takes us back to the lessons learned from *Experiencing*

God. If you want to be led by the Spirit, you need to spend time—daily time—praying and studying your Bible. You will not be able to get by with only an occasional glance at the Bible and a hurried prayer.

Essentials for Hearing God's voice

When you start to spend daily time going empty-handed to God in prayer, God's voice will begin to stand out. As this happens, you'll start recognizing that some of the thoughts that come to your mind when you pray are thoughts coming from God. With time, as you start paying more attention, you'll get better at recognizing which thoughts are really God's voice speaking to you.

The same will happen as you commit yourself to daily Bible study. Over time you will begin to see how the things you've recently read apply directly to things happening in your life. Soon you'll be reading the Bible with eager anticipation, wondering how the Spirit will use it to lead and prepare you for unexpected opportunities.

Do you get the point? Prayer and Bible study are essential to being led by the Spirit. However, there are two additional things that are also important. First, when you sense God is saying something to you, check it out with trusted friends who have proven to be sensitive to the Spirit's leading. These people can help you discern between wishful thoughts and God's voice. This is practicing Proverbs 11:14 which says, "For lack of guidance a nation falls, but many advisers make victory sure."

The second thing you'll need to do is to take a risk and act on what you're sensing from God. The Spirit cannot lead you if you will not follow. The advice of James applies here: "Do not merely listen to the word… Do what it says!" (James 1:22).

I want to be absolutely clear. If you want to be led by the Spirit, there's no avoiding this process of daily Bible study, prayer, spiritual counsel and action. Until you start doing these things, your time in the wilderness will be wasted. If you want to learn the lessons God has for you in the wilderness, you need to get started on these things. And you need to start NOW!

Chapter Four

When God Puts You On Hold, Don't Hang Up!

"So don't get tired of doing what is good. Don't get discouraged and give up, for we will reap a harvest of blessing at the appropriate time."
Galatians 6:9 (NLT)

I pressed "1" for English. Next, I pressed "3" for account information. I kept pressing buttons as I worked through the phone tree, but I wasn't getting answers to my questions. So finally, in frustration, I pressed "0." A recorded voice came on the line and said, "Please remain on the line and your call will be answered in the order in which it was received." I had to make a choice. I could stay on the line, hang up and try again, or I could throw the phone across the room. It was a close call, but I stayed on the line. I knew that if I hung up and called again I'd only get moved to the end of the line and have to start the process all over again.

There are times in life when it feels like God has put you on hold. These are wilderness times and during these times you have to make a choice. Either you can hang in there, or you can hang up on God and smash your future against the wall. I'm praying you choose not to hang up.

Snagglepuss Christians

Do you remember Snagglepuss? He's an old TV cartoon character whose famous line whenever things got tough was, "Exit, stage left." I see a lot of Snagglepuss Christians in America. When God throws them a curve ball, they "Exit, stage left."

We are people in a hurry. We're in a rush to be successful. When we struggle, we want immediate deliverance. If God doesn't act on our timetable, we assume He needs help. So we try to manipulate our own miracle and direct our own deliverance.

When that doesn't work, we conclude that God must not care. That's when we start to pull back from our Christian friends, drop out of serving, and worship less frequently. We may even quit worshiping altogether. It seems God has dropped us, so we drop him. We exit, stage left.

You'll Learn More through Delay than through Deliverance

The problem is that we belong to a culture that hates delay. Corporations expect immediate results and so do our churches. Delay is viewed as a bad thing, and when there is a delay, we assume someone has failed. When a church faces a delay they'll often say, "the devil must be at work." But I don't see this in the Bible. I see the opposite. I see delay as a biblical theme.

The Bible is filled with examples of people that God put on hold.

- Noah was told to build an ark—but it was as many as 100 years before the flood came.
- Abraham was told he would become the father of nations—but he waited 25 years before his elderly wife conceived.
- David was anointed as the next king of Israel—but he had to wait 15 years before he was appointed king.
- Isaiah prophesied about a coming Messiah—but it was 700 years before Jesus came.
- Jesus was baptized and ready to fulfill his purpose—but the Spirit took him into the wilderness for 40 days before He began His public ministry.
- The Apostle Paul had a powerful conversion experience—but he spent years in obscurity before Barnabas found Paul and helped him launch his ministry.
- Jesus promised to come again—but 2,000 years later we still wait expectantly for that moment to come.

Delay is a common theme in the Bible. We should expect it, but I don't know many people who do. Most of us want success—and we want it NOW! We want answers—and we want them NOW! We want to be delivered—and we want it NOW! But thanks be to God that He loves us too much to give us what we want—NOW.

The truth is that we will learn more from delay than deliverance. God has important lessons to teach us, lessons we will never learn if He instantly delivers us. We need this time of delay for God to prepare us so we'll be ready when it's "show time."

The Main Event

Have you ever heard of an "undercard" in boxing? The undercards are a series of matches between lesser boxers before the Main Event. They're the openers who get the crowd excited and pumped up.

The truth is that we will learn more from delay than deliverance.

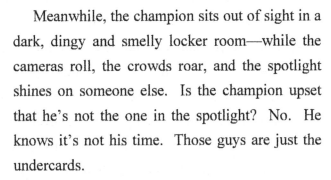

Meanwhile, the champion sits out of sight in a dark, dingy and smelly locker room—while the cameras roll, the crowds roar, and the spotlight shines on someone else. Is the champion upset that he's not the one in the spotlight? No. He knows it's not his time. Those guys are just the undercards.

While the undercards are in the spotlight, the champion prepares for the Main Event. He gets loosened up. His hands are carefully taped while he listens to his trainer's instructions. Although he's heard these instructions over and over before, the champ continues to listen. He repeats the instructions in his mind because he doesn't want to forget them when the announcer says, "Ladies and gentlemen, announcing the Main Event."

When we find ourselves sitting out of sight, we need to understand that God is using that time to prepare us. There are lessons we must learn in order to be ready for the Main Event. There are unhealthy things that God must strip from our lives. We must strengthen our trust in God. We must drill God's instructions into our minds until we learn how to instinctively follow His ways. We need to spend enough time with God that we will hear His voice through the roar of the crowd. We must learn how to take a hit and still stand firm in tough times.

Unfortunately, too often we get upset when we hear the crowds roaring for someone else while we're sitting in the shadows. Instead of waiting, we give up on God's plan. We exit, stage left. We miss the Main Event.

Exit, Stage Left

Earl is one of those guys who missed the Main Event. I first met Earl when he came up to me after a speaking engagement and said, "I really need your help. I need to change my lifestyle." Earl convinced me that he desperately wanted to break free from the destructive lifestyle he was living and was willing to do whatever was necessary to change.

I gave Earl a set of steps he would need to act on if he was serious about allowing God to transform his life, and I walked with him through each one. I watched with joy as Earl's life drastically changed for the better.

Earl obediently committed himself to following Christ, and I could see the call of God on his life. When he ministered to people, I sensed the presence of God working. When he prayed, things would happen and folks would get healed. When he sang, I felt chills. He was not faking. He was not posturing. You could tell that God had worked a miracle in his life and was starting to use him.

If you're a great preacher, if people get chills when you sing, and if things happen when you pray, then usually there's going to be a spot for you. You're on the fast track for success. But that wasn't happening for Earl. Even though he was a part of our ministry, he wasn't "prime time." At least not yet.

Because Earl had committed himself to obedience, God had taken him to the wilderness. God wanted to strengthen his character so that he would be ready for the Main Event. What Earl needed to do was wait patiently for God to establish his ministry. The waiting would build his character and strengthen his trust in God.

But for Earl, things weren't happening fast enough. He didn't enjoy ministering in the background. Instead of waiting on God, Earl began to slip, and he lapsed into sexual sin.

Here was this wonderful guy who had experienced God. He had the call of God on his life. He had a wonderful future in front of him, but he was blowing it with his impatience. So I looked Earl in the eye and had a heart-to-heart talk about the bad choices he was making. I challenged him to wait on God's timing.

Unfortunately, even as I talked I could see that Earl wasn't going to heed my warnings. Instead, he chose to exit, stage left. Earl left our church and went to another ministry. Soon afterwards, he had a major moral failure and landed in prison.

Hebrews 11:25-26 says that Moses "chose to be mistreated along with the people of God rather than to enjoy the pleasures of sin for a short time. He regarded disgrace for the sake of Christ as of greater value than the treasures of Egypt, because he was looking ahead to his reward."

Earl did the opposite. He chose moments of pleasure rather than suffer God's delay for the sake of his future. All Earl needed to do was walk through the wilderness, but he failed to understand the purpose of the waiting. He didn't realize that it wasn't his time yet—God was preparing him for the Main Event. Instead, Earl exited, stage left. He hung up on God. He missed the Main Event.

Shortcuts Out of the Wilderness

The wilderness can be long and painful. We don't know when it will end. We feel isolated and afraid. And most often we just want relief. This is when we can get into trouble and start looking for a shortcut. Earl's shortcut was moments of sinful pleasure, but there are other shortcuts as well.

The Shortcut of Bitterness

Maybe your wilderness is the result of a tragedy or some misfortune. You've lost a loved one, a job, a retirement fund or your health. You feel out of control and out of options. If you were directing your life, this is not the way you'd have it play out.

This is when you have a choice. Will you stay close to God in this wilderness of misfortune—or will you take the shortcut of bitterness? Will you lean on God and allow Him to help you navigate your grief—or will you rehearse your problems over and over, giving in to a pity party? Will you choose to trust that God is good and in control—or will you flip the script and take the shortcut of bitterness, letting it poison your life?

The Shortcut of Separation

Maybe your wilderness is the result of a tough season in your marriage. You feel unappreciated. You and your spouse are not on the same page. You argue all the time, or worse, you don't even communicate at all. You feel isolated and lonely in your relationship, and see no hope of change on the horizon.

This is when you have a choice. Will you trust God to bring new life to a broken marriage—or will you take the shortcut of divorce? Will you let God heal the broken places in your heart—or will you emotionally check out of your marriage? Will you be faithful to God and to your marriage covenant—or will you give in to the pressure and exit the scene?

The Shortcut of A Wrong Relationship

Maybe your wilderness is the result of being single and wishing you were married. It seems like other people are able to find that special someone, but you're still on your own. You imagine how happy and fulfilled you would be if only "Mr. Right" or "Ms. Wonderful" would walk into your life. You've been waiting your whole life, and the wait is getting too hard and too long.

This is when you have a choice. Will you allow God to teach you to fall in love with Him—or will you jump into an ill-advised relationship? Will you allow God to fill your lonely heart—or will you take the relationship-fast-track and pursue a convenient marriage that's not going to last? Will you wait on God—or will you rush into a relational shortcut that's doomed to leave your heart broken?

These are not shortcuts, they are short-circuits. Even though they provide temporary relief, they will cause more heartache and pain than any trial you'll ever experience in the wilderness. I can't say this strongly enough—don't give in to the temptation of a shortcut. Embrace the wilderness, and allow God to do a work in your life that will produce fruit.

Don't Hang Up

You don't go to bed a blunder and wake up a wonder! It takes time for God to shape you and strengthen you for the Main Event. There are lessons you must first learn in the wilderness.

There will be times in ministry or in business when you know you could do more but you don't have the opportunity—hang in there! There will be times when others are getting all the praise even though they're not doing half as much as you—hang in there! There will be times when you're doing all the right things yet seem to be getting nowhere—hang in there! You're not the undercard. God is preparing you for the Main Event!

You don't go to bed a blunder and wake up a wonder!

Second Chances

Earl's out of prison now. He has turned back to God, and God has brought him back to the wilderness. However, the road through the wilderness has become longer for Earl because he now carries the burden of being a convicted felon. That's the problem with hanging up on God and trying to take your own shortcut. You'll still end up back in the wilderness, but you'll be further behind than you were before.

The good news is that God can minister powerfully through Earl again if he sticks out the wilderness this time. If you've hung up on God, you can get back on the line as well. God has not given up on you, or on the plans He has for you, but you'll need to go back to the wilderness and give God as much time as He needs to prepare you for the Main Event.

Better yet—don't hang up on God at all. Then, you won't have to make up the time recovering from your mistakes. The lesson you need to learn is that your time in the wilderness has a purpose. God is preparing you to be a champion. So, when God puts you on hold, DON'T HANG UP!

Chapter Five

You Can't Fake The Funk

"Do not think of yourself more highly than you ought,
but rather think of yourself with sober judgment."
Romans 12:3

When I was a young pastor, I thought that I had "arrived," but I discovered that I was just "faking the funk."

Success or Significance?

The church I led at that time had all the glamorous programs that catch people's attention. We were well known in the community. We were on television and radio. We served the community with food, health and youth programs. We were a success. But I'm not so sure that we were significant.

Do you know the difference between success and significance? Success focuses on external things. It's about how you appear to others. Significance, on the other hand, focuses on eternal things. It's about how you appear to God, how God is changing your life and how God is using you to change the lives of others.

I witnessed this "success vs. significance" principle in action one day when I walked in on our church's food program. The purpose of this program was to serve the needy, but I couldn't believe what I saw. Our people weren't ministering to the folks, they were fussing at them. Even worse, our people were keeping some of the best food for themselves. I was embarrassed. It should never have happened that way.

There was a gap between what our church looked like and who we really were. On the outside we looked good. We looked like we were sharing Christ's love. But on the inside, we were just doing our duty—with very little love or compassion. Although we looked successful, we weren't being significant. The food program wasn't changing lives because our own lives didn't exhibit the transformation God's presence brings. That's what I call "faking the funk." It's pretending to be better than you really are. But God sees the difference. You can't fake the funk with God.

Looking Good

The truth is we're all susceptible to faking the funk because we want to be seen as successful. So, we earn degrees, hang certificates on the wall, collect trophies, gain promotions and pick up titles. We buy nice homes, cars, and clothes. We're on the church board and belong to the Chamber of Commerce. We usher at church, teach Sunday school, lead a Bible study or even preach. We pray out loud. We quote Bible verses. We tithe our income. We look good, really good. We look successful.

So, what's wrong with doing those things? Absolutely nothing! It's all good. The danger lies in believing that we're significant simply because we do those things.

We believe that we're something special because we have more degrees than a thermometer. We believe that we're important because we have titles and sit in boardrooms. We believe that lives are being changed because our churches have the latest programs. We believe we've earned God's favor because we pray frequently, read our Bibles regularly, give generously, and volunteer willingly.

Because we look like a success, we believe we're significant, but the one does not equal the other. There's a difference between looking good and being good—and God sees the difference.

Modern-day Pharisees

When we fake the funk, we're in danger of focusing on what we want to do externally over what God wants to do eternally. We're in danger of listening to the praise of men over the voice of God. We're in danger of trusting the power of success over the power of God. When we fake the funk, we're in danger of becoming modern-day Pharisees.

The Pharisees of the Bible looked good, really good. They prayed. They studied Scripture. They tithed. They religiously kept all the rules. They were leaders. They were respected. They were successful—but they weren't significant. They weren't changing lives because the presence of God hadn't changed their lives. They weren't filled with the Spirit because they were too full of themselves.

Jesus aimed his sharpest words at the false spirituality of the Pharisees. In Matthew 23, Jesus calls them "fools," "blind guides," "hypocrites" and "whitewashed tombs, which look beautiful on the outside but on the inside are full of dead men's bones and everything unclean." *That's not good.*

Whether we want to admit it or not, we can become Pharisees. We can focus on the trappings of personal, professional and spiritual success and think we've made it—we've won God's favor. Just like the Pharisees, we mistake success for significance. When that happens, we become so full of ourselves that there's no room to be filled with the Spirit. *That's not good.*

We become so full of ourselves that there's no room to be filled with the Spirit.

A Warning

The Apostle Paul warns us of the danger of faking the funk with God. In Romans 12:3 Paul says, "Because of the privilege and the authority God has given me, I give you this warning: Don't think you are better than you really are. Be honest in your evaluation of yourself. Measure yourself by the faith God has given you" (NLT).

Paul was speaking from experience. He was once a proud, deluded Pharisee who had all the trappings of success. He had the pedigree. He was the protégé of the famous Pharisee, Gamaliel. He was a faultless rule keeper. He was a rising star. But all that stuff got in the way of his being able to recognize the work of God.

On the outside Paul looked good, really good—but on the inside he was opposing what God was doing. Paul was faking the funk, and he didn't even know it. His success and false spirituality had blinded him. But God got his attention.

Just like Paul, you can be faking the funk without even knowing it. But God will get your attention. He will break you away from your daily routine and take you to the wilderness where there's no hiding, it's just you and God.

When Our Character Needs Strengthening

That's what happened to my friend Earl. Remember Earl from the last chapter? Because he was listening to the praise of men, he thought he was ready for "prime time," but God wasn't bringing those opportunities his way. Instead of waiting, Earl tried to make things happen on his own. His impatience proved to be disastrous.

After Earl got out of prison, I asked him what he'd learned from what happened. He told me that he realized that prior to prison he didn't have a strong enough character for sustained ministry. Although God wanted to strengthen his character, Earl admitted that he had been unwilling to give God the time to do so. The result? His inner character wasn't strong enough to support his outer success, and he crashed.

Remember the words of Paul in Romans 12:3? He said, "Don't think you are better than you really are. Be honest in your evaluation of yourself." Well, Earl thought he was better than he really was. It took a severe wilderness experience before Earl took an honest evaluation of himself and allowed God to start rebuilding his character.

When "Success" Gets in the Way

The church I led was faking the funk too. We had all the trappings of success—the TV and radio programs and community outreach ministries. But the danger is that you can miss a new work of God because you're unwilling to let go of the things you already have—the trappings of success. That was the danger our church faced, but God took care of it. He just didn't take away our programs, He took away our building.

When we lost our lease and "temporarily" moved in with Harvest Church, we had to halt our T.V. and radio ministries as well as our health and food programs—all the things that made us look successful. Although these were good things, they had become roadblocks to experiencing a new work of God. If God hadn't stripped them away, we never would have been available for God to do a miracle.

After that miracle, I discovered that I had been faking the funk as well. When our two churches merged, everything that gave me my sense of identity was stripped away. I was no longer preaching or the pastor of a church. I was no longer seen as a leader in the community. I no longer heard the praise of people. I wasn't even the bread winner in my family anymore. I no longer knew who I was. But God knew who I was and He took me to the wilderness to show me.

Not as Good as I Thought

In the wilderness, God stripped away all the things that made me look successful, and I discovered that I wasn't as good as I thought I was. I had character flaws that God needed to fix before He could do a new work through me.

Not as Good of a Husband

First, I found out that I wasn't as good of a husband as I thought. I thought I was a great husband because I was committed to Charlene, and we looked like a happy couple. However, I had been too busy with my ministry success to notice that I was ignoring my wife's feelings and disregarding her input.

The truth finally hit me one day when my loving wife grabbed the kids and walked out—without speaking to me. I realized that something was terribly amiss. It wasn't until she walked out of the house that I realized who was at fault—me.

Charlene had warned me about a woman she believed was interested in me romantically. Although Charlene had tried to tell me that I was misreading this woman's intentions, I dismissed her and told her she was overreacting. Big mistake!

I shut her down. I was insensitive to her feelings. I disregarded her keen insight into this other woman who, it turned out, was indeed pursuing me. If I had continued faking the funk as a husband, it would have been a disaster for my marriage.

Thankfully, God took me to the wilderness so that I could face the truth about myself. God transformed me into a better husband, and now I listen more carefully to Charlene's opinions and perceptions, and I'm more sensitive to her feelings. I am a better man and a better husband because of it.

Not as Good of Papa

I also discovered that I wasn't being a very good dad to my son and daughter. Technically, they are my step kids, but I don't look at them that way—I never have. When Charlene and I were married, they became my son and daughter. The problem was that we were married while I was in the midst of being a busy, successful pastor. When that busy life was stripped away, I discovered that I didn't know my kids well. In fact, I'm embarrassed to admit that for several months my son Anthony called me "Bishop" instead of "Papa." I wasn't yet significant in the lives of my children.

In the wilderness I had plenty of time on my hands, and I used it to start becoming "Papa" to my family instead of "Bishop." We went through some bumps in our family life as I strived to become a better dad but, in the end, the wilderness was a gift that made us a strong family. If I had stayed the busy pastor, my "successful" ministry would have crushed my family, and I wouldn't have seen the truth until it was too late.

Not as Good of a Person

The next thing God showed me in the wilderness was that doing good things didn't make me a good person. God taught me this lesson by bringing to my attention the way I used to handle my relationships with women when I was a bachelor. I never technically "dated" women; I simply befriended them in close ways. Externally, I did the right things. I was always a gentleman and I adhered to the Bible's teaching about relationships with women. But that doesn't mean I was good.

I allowed women to believe things about the relationship that weren't true. As a result, they would get hurt when I would stop pursuing the relationship. To everyone else, I looked okay. It looked like I was doing everything right, but in reality I was leaving a trail of broken hearts. *That wasn't good.*

This was a character flaw that needed to be fixed. Even after I was married and dating was no longer an issue, I still needed to grow in the way I communicated with others. How could God use me to minister to people if I hurt them because I allowed them to have wrong impressions and expectations of me?

Not as Good of a Christian

God then showed me that I was doing the same thing with Him. In my relationship with God, I was doing the right things—praying, reading the Bible, giving, obeying—but I wasn't giving God my heart. I used the spiritual disciplines as if they were a math equation. Bible + prayer + obedience = God's favor. I did these things because that's what "successful" Christians are supposed to do. Instead of using spiritual practices to get closer to God's heart, I used them as a way to look good in God's eyes and earn His favor. So, although I was doing good things, I wasn't good. I was breaking God's heart.

But then, God broke my faulty equation. In the wilderness, I no longer experienced God's favor—at least not the kind of favor I expected—even though I was doing all the right things. However, once my faulty thinking was broken, God was able to teach me the real purpose of spiritual practices such as prayer, Bible study, giving, and obedience.

I learned that I am to pray, read, give and obey for no other reason than because God is worthy of my full attention and commitment. I learned that spiritual disciplines have nothing to do with earning favor from God or being successful. The disciplines are about being faithful no matter what happens. The purpose of spiritual disciplines is to allow me to grow closer to God's heart and to allow God to enter my heart and transform it.

This was an invaluable lesson. Because I had been faking the funk with my practice of spiritual disciplines, my relationship with God was threatened and I didn't even realize it. In the wilderness, God stripped away my false spirituality so that He could strengthen and rebuild my character.

You Can't Fake the Funk In The Wilderness

As I look back on my wilderness experience, I can see that God had a plan for me. There was a new work that He wanted me to do, but my character wasn't strong enough yet. I had character flaws that needed to be addressed otherwise my marriage, family and ministry would be destroyed by my "success."

However, because I was faking the funk, I couldn't see my flaws. That's why God took me to the wilderness. It was there that God showed me who I really was. Seeing the truth about myself was painful but necessary. Once this happened, I was able to confess my failures and allow God to transform me into who He knew I could be.

You're Not as Good as You Think You Are

God has plans for all of us, but before we can step into those plans and experience His power, our character needs to be strengthened. The reality is: you are not as good as you think you are. There are flaws in your character that God needs to address so that you can go forward. Otherwise, your success will crush you. When you are faking the funk, God will not work in your life since you are too full of yourself to be filled with the Spirit.

Because God loves you, He will take you to the wilderness to strip away your false spirituality, your false reliance on success, and your false belief that you are better than you really are. It is there that you'll discover the truth about who you really are, and it won't be pretty. But this is good because once you face the truth you can allow God to deal with it. Once you see your weaknesses, you can allow God to strengthen them. Once you stop focusing on being a "success," you can allow God to make you significant.

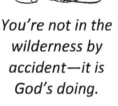

You're not in the wilderness by accident—it is God's doing.

So when you find yourself in the wilderness, here's what I want you to understand: You're not there by accident—this is God's doing. He has plans for you. But first there are things God needs to strip away from your life, and there are weaknesses in your character that God needs to strengthen.

A Wilderness Action Plan

When you're in the wilderness, here's what you can do to cooperate with God's work in your life:

1. Heed the warning of Romans 12:3. "Don't think you are better than you really are. Be honest in your evaluation of yourself. Measure yourself by the faith God has given you." So, instead of stewing over all the things that have been taken away, focus on who you are without those things. Take an <u>honest evaluation</u> of yourself—even though it might not be pretty.

2. Go butt-naked before God. As God reveals how you've

been faking the funk, <u>confess those failures</u>. He already knows who you really are, and He knows who you can be. You're the one who won't admit the truth. Confession releases God's power to transform you. Until you recognize who you really are, God can't transform you into who you can be.

3. Keep praying, reading your Bible and being obedient. I've known too many people who have done the opposite. Their spiritual disciplines didn't seem to work. They didn't get the results they expected. So, they think: *"Why keep wasting time praying or studying if the wilderness is my reward?"* These people quit on God and miss out on the significant new work He wanted to do in their lives.

   You've got to understand that spiritual disciplines don't earn favor from God. That's not why you do them. You do them because God is worthy of your full attention no matter what. They will allow you to pull closer to God's heart, and give God entrance to your heart as well.

   In the wilderness, the disciplines will be your lifeline. God will use your practice of prayer, study and obedience to reveal the truth about who you are and transform your life.

When You Stop Faking the Funk God Can Do Great Things

God took me to the wilderness to get me to stop faking the funk. God will take you into the wilderness for the same reason. When He does, you may not like what you learn. But if you embrace the truth, God will do great things in your life.

Chapter Six

Gotta Have Ya

"Blessed are the poor in spirit,

for theirs is the kingdom of heaven."

Matthew 5:3

When our church moved in with Harvest Church it was almost like going to another planet. And worshiping there, well—do you know that old saying, "I don't think we're in Kansas anymore?" That's how it felt at first.

I grew up in the black gospel tradition. We sang songs accompanied by the keyboard, piano, bass, drums and, of course, the Hammond B3 organ. If you didn't have a Hammond B3, then it just wasn't happening. Harvest Church had a B3, but they didn't use it the way I was accustomed to.

A Worship Wilderness

They didn't sing songs with "style" at Harvest Church either—at least not the style I preferred. They did something called "contemporary praise music" and sprinkled in some R&B once and awhile. I didn't know most of the songs they sang. They sang songs like, "I'm Trading My Sorrows." What was that about?

After attending Harvest for two months, I found that I was still uncomfortable with their style of worship; in fact, secretly, I often found myself complaining and wishing for my old gospel music.

Around that time, I took my family on a road trip to visit relatives. It was a 2,000 mile trip, and we only brought three music tapes. As we drove out of the driveway, I put in my gospel music, and I was in heaven. I was worshiping the way God intended.

But after listening to my music, my wife wanted to play her tape. Wouldn't you know it, her music turned out to be the same praise songs we sang at church. I couldn't believe it. I thought I had escaped that. But I wasn't going to spend two weeks in a car with an unhappy wife. After all, happy wife—happy life. So my wife's tape went in and out of the speakers came the song "I'm Trading my Sorrows."

Where's My Joy?

A surprising thing happened. For the first time I didn't hear the music. I heard the words. As I listened to "I'm trading my sorrows...I'm laying them down for the joy of the Lord," I started asking myself, "Where does my joy come from?" If it came from having a church, I was in trouble. If it came from preaching, I was in trouble. If it came from a certain style of worship, I was in trouble. I no longer had any of those things.

I realized that instead of experiencing joy, I'd been grumbling about the songs we sang in church. They weren't my style. Then I thought of all the messages I had preached about joy not coming from having stuff but from having a real relationship with God.

God was speaking to my spirit. He was telling me: "I brought you to the wilderness to let you know that you don't need to have a church. You don't need to preach. You don't need to have 'your' music. But you gotta have ME!"

You can do the math—a two week road trip and only three tapes. Can you imagine how many times I heard the song "I'm Trading My Sorrows?" And each time I heard the words, "I'm trading my sorrows…I'm laying them down for the joy of the Lord," God was driving home this lesson: "If you want joy, you don't have to have anything else, but ya gotta have Me."

BrylCreem God

It's embarrassing to admit, but as a pastor I had treated God like that old hair product, Brylcreem. Remember their slogan, "A little dab will do ya?" It wasn't that I was ignoring God. I truly wanted to be God's man, and I truly believed I was being fully dependent on Him. But the reality was I'd come to rely on other things like our church's programs and style—more than I knew.

Our church's programs were good. They were doing good things. The problem was that I couldn't imagine being successful without them. I had unknowingly created a formula that went like this: our programs plus a dab of God would bring success.

I needed to learn how much I relied on other things in addition to God before He could take me forward in accomplishing His plans for my life. So, God took me to the wilderness to show me that I didn't need a certain music style to help me get closer to

Him. I didn't need certain programs to effectively serve Him. What I needed, more than anything, was God alone.

Blessed are Those Desperate for God

In Matthew 5:3, Jesus teaches us that "God blesses those who realize their need for Him, for the Kingdom of God is given to them" (NLT). I like how *The Message* version paraphrases that verse: "You're blessed when you are at the end of your rope. With less of you there is more of God."

There's no getting around what Jesus is saying here. He's clear and direct. Jesus wants everyone to know that the best place to be is in a place where you're desperate for God. God will bless those who are desperate for Him.

God will take you to the wilderness to get you to a place where you gotta have God, or there's no way you'll survive. Once you get to that place of desperation, you'll experience for yourself that God is all you need. That will be a life-changing moment.

Now you'll have strength that comes from deep within you. It's a strength that comes from the peace you have regardless of the circumstances, because you know that God is all you need. It's the strength of an inner confidence that says, "I can handle anything that comes at me because I know that God is all I need."

Now you're totally available to God. You know you can do anything that God asks of you because you know that God is all you need to get it done. Now you're ready to let God do anything He chooses to do through you—even a miracle. If God can accomplish this in your life, then the wilderness will be worth it.

The "What I Need to Succeed" List

I don't mean no harm, but most of us like to think that we're totally dependent on God. We're not. We have a list in our heads of what we think we need in order to be successful in serving God.

For example, most of us would put "having a paycheck" on our list of "What I Need to Succeed." And not just any paycheck—we have a certain dollar amount in our heads that we believe we "must" have to live. Further, we believe we need a special kind of education or a certain type of skill in order to serve God, so that's on our list, too. Then, in order to worship God we feel we need a certain kind of music and a certain kind of atmosphere. So we put that on our list as well.

I don't mean no harm, but most of us like to think that we're totally dependent on God. We're not.

I know pastors who won't start new churches unless they have a Media Team. I know business people who sense God calling them to become pastors, until they find out it means a pay cut. I know folks who come late to church because they don't like the music. We all think we are totally dependent on God, but we have our lists of what we need to succeed. If we don't have the things on our list, we won't step out from our comfort zones, and we wonder why we don't experience more God-moments.

"God, I Gotta Have Ya"

God will take you to the wilderness to show you that you have a "What I Need to Succeed" list. Then He will make that list worthless. In the wilderness God will start removing the things that are on your list. It might be your paycheck. It might be your health.

It might be your friends, activities, programs, or even your cherished worship music. It will be the things you think you need, things that you rely on even more than God, but maybe you don't realize it.

In the wilderness, everything you thought you needed will be taken away. That's when you'll have to make a choice. You can "Exit, stage left" and miss out on the new work God has planned for you. Or you can enter "God Territory" where you become desperate and cry out, "God, I gotta have ya or I won't make it."

Entering "God Territory"

In Judges 6-8, we see God doing this very thing with His chosen people, the children of Israel. God was allowing Israel to be oppressed by a group called the Midianites. Things got so bad that Israel finally cried out to God for relief and God's answer was Gideon.

Gideon wouldn't have been on anyone's list of people most likely to succeed. He was the weakest member of the smallest clan of his tribe. He was so insecure that he put out his infamous fleece and asked God to prove to him, twice, that God was making the right choice in asking him to lead the Israelites.

Finally convinced, Gideon mustered up an army of 32,000 warriors to face a Midianite force that the Bible says were "as thick as locusts." The odds were against Israel, but God was going to show His people that He alone was all they needed.

God instructed Gideon to reduce his army by 99% and then arm them, not with swords, but with jars, torches, and trumpets. This strategy would not make anyone's list of "How to Succeed in

Battle." Gideon was now in God Territory. Gideon had to make a choice: either he could choose to be totally dependent on God, or he could say it wouldn't work and run away.

You probably know the rest of the story. Gideon trusted in God alone, and God did not disappoint! Three hundred men using nothing but jars and trumpets routed the Midianite army. Israel learned that God was all they needed. Although Gideon didn't have anything you would put on a list of things needed to succeed, he stepped out of his comfort zone, entered God Territory and God did a miracle.

I don't know if God has a miracle planned for you; however, I do know that God has a limitless supply of miracles. He does not need to ration them. He does not need to hold miracles back in case He needs one later. So, God may very well have a miracle in store for you. But He will not do that miracle until you are able to throw away your "What I Need To Succeed" list and say, "God is all I need."

Flat Broke At KFC

In order to get me to the place where I knew that God was all I needed, He took me to the point of desperation several times. One of those times happened at an unlikely place—the local KFC.

You often hear people say that they don't have *any* money. But what they really mean is that they don't have any *spare* money. Well, Charlene and I got to a point where we literally had NO money: zero, zilch, nada, nothing.

One day, we were on our way to minister to some friends who had been going through a difficult time in their lives. We wanted to bless them by bringing them a meal and spending some time praying with them. On our way to their house, we stopped at KFC to pick up a meal of chicken, mashed potatoes, biscuits and cole-slaw.

"I'm sorry, sir," the cashier said, "but your credit card won't accept the charge."

The words hit me like a ton of bricks. In a mixture of despera-tion and hope, I said, "Try punching in the numbers. Maybe the magnetic strip on the card isn't working."

She tried again, but the credit card was maxed out. I tried an-other card but had the same results. The reality of the situation be-gan to hit me. I had no money in the bank to write a check. I had no cash in my wallet or even in my house, and now I couldn't even use my credit cards. This meant I was flat broke—almost.

We went out to our car and pulled up the floor mats and checked in every nook and cranny. We finally managed to scrounge up enough coins to pay for the chicken—but *only* the chicken. Now we were flat broke. We didn't even have enough money to buy a biscuit. We were at the "God, we gotta have ya or we won't make it" point.

We brought our meager offering of chicken to our friends. They wondered where the biscuits were but they appreciated the gesture. Because we were there to care for our friends, we didn't mention our financial struggles; instead, we had a great evening of encouraging and praying for them.

When it was time for us to leave, they said they'd like to do something to bless us in return, so they handed us a check for

$100. My breath caught in my throat. Charlene and I looked at each other, knowing that this money was a direct gift from God. You would have thought it was a million dollars for the intensity of joy I felt. In my heart, I was jumping up and down saying, "Thank you, Jesus!"

In our wilderness, God had allowed us to come to a place where our resources were exhausted. All we had left was Him. Now, God was showing us that He was all we needed.

Free from Nagging Doubt

You have probably heard that God is all you need. You may even think you believe that God is all you need. But until you experience it for yourself, there's always that nagging doubt.

God had allowed us to come to a place where our resources were exhausted. All we had left was Him.

It's that nagging doubt that can get you in trouble. It's the nagging doubt that prevents you from experiencing God-moments. It's the nagging doubt that keeps you from following the Spirit to do something unheard of—like attacking a vast army with a jar and a trumpet.

God takes us to the wilderness to remove the nagging doubt. God wants us to experience for ourselves that He is all we need. So He takes us to a place where He is all we have.

Do you realize how liberating it is to be freed from the nagging doubt? Your fear is removed. Courage is gained. You no longer *think* God can do anything, you *know* God can do anything. Best of all, you know God can do anything *through you.*

Once you are free from your list of "Things I Need to Succeed," you will no longer be held back from doing the work God has planned for you. Because you have experienced for yourself that all you need is God, you will no longer insist on having the things on your list before you follow God.

Ready for Anything

I always thought that I was totally dependent on God, but God used the wilderness to show me differently. It was there that I realized I had a list of things I needed besides God. And it was there that God destroyed that list.

God led me to give up my church and then He took away my preaching, my music, and my money. God took me to a place where I cried out, "I gotta have ya God, or I will die in this wilderness."

That experience changed my life. If God hadn't destroyed my list, if I hadn't experienced that God was all I needed, I would have never stepped out to the new work He had planned for me. I would have never seen the miracles I've experienced since then.

God wants to do the same for you. God will take you into the wilderness. When He does, stay there. Allow yourself to get to the point where you are desperate and you have to cry out, "God, I gotta have ya or I won't make it!" That's when you will find out for yourself that God is all you need. Once you get there, you'll be ready for anything.

Chapter Seven

Do You Really Know God?

"What is more, I consider everything a loss compared to the surpassing greatness of knowing Christ Jesus my Lord.... I want to know Christ and the power of his resurrection and the fellowship of sharing in his sufferings."
Philippians 3:8,10

Over the last decade, one of America's favorite television series has been *CSI: Crime Scene Investigation.* Millions of people watch each week as forensic investigators find seemingly insignificant clues—a fiber here, a crumb there, a scuff mark—and then can say with confidence, "This is what really happened."

Today's churches are filled with "forensic Christians." After God has acted, we can look back, see the evidence of God's work and say with confidence, "God was there." It's easy to recognize where God has been. What I want to know is where are the people who can recognize where God is going? Where are the believers who can say, "This is the way God wants us to go?" Where are the ones at the forefront of what God is doing instead of trying to catch up to it?

Something is Wrong

On the night Barak Obama was elected president, a quarter-million people of every race packed Grant Park in Chicago to celebrate the election of our first African-American president. As I watched that historic moment on television, I had the thought that this is what one nation under God looks like.

When I look at the American Church, however, that's not what I see. I see the black church, the white church, and the brown church. What is this? If all races can join together to celebrate an election, why can't we join together to worship God?

There is no question that reconciliation is the clarion call of God. Through Jesus Christ, God took decisive action to reconcile all races to each other and to Him. That was 2,000 years ago. So why isn't the Church out in front on the issue of racial unity? Why aren't we serving as ambassadors of racial reconciliation? Why aren't there more multi-ethnic congregations? Why is our nation ahead of the church in diversity rather than the other way around?

When it comes to racial reconciliation, something is wrong—the Church is not at the forefront of what God is doing. There are too few who are saying, "This is where God is going, and we need to join Him."

Knowing God's Ways

Our churches are filled with people who say they believe in God; in fact, most Americans say they believe in God. There is a difference, however, between *believing in* God and *knowing* God and His ways. This difference can be seen between Moses and the Israelites. Psalm 103:7 says God "made known His *ways* to Moses,

His *acts* to the children of Israel" (NKJV).

Moses arrived in Egypt telling the children of Israel, "God is going to set you free." The people said, "Who are you?" Then they saw God act by changing Pharaoh's hard heart.

When Pharaoh released them, Moses said, "This is the direction." The people said, "You crazy fool, we're trapped." Then they saw God act by parting the Red Sea.

After crossing through the Red Sea, Moses said, "The Promised Land is this way." The people said, "We'll starve going that way." Then they saw God act by providing manna each day.

Our churches—our world—need more believers who can say, "This is what God wants us to do."

The children of Israel saw the acts of God and could say after the fact, "That was God." But Moses knew God's ways and could say before the fact, "This is what God is doing. This is where God is going." That's the difference between believing in God and knowing God's ways.

Our churches—our world—need more believers who can say, "This is what God wants us to do." Our Lord Jesus Christ wants you to be that kind of person. Jesus makes it clear, "My sheep listen to my voice; I know them, and they follow me" (John 10:27). Jesus wants us to recognize His voice and follow Him—before the fact, not after the act.

A Matter of Life and Death

Recognizing and following Jesus' voice before you see Him act requires sensitivity and faith. If you don't develop that sensitivity, you'll never recognize Jesus' voice; and if you don't build the faith, you'll never follow Him to the new places He wants to take you. That's bad, but it gets worse.

In ancient times, sheep had to leave the pen to get fed and watered. So, if sheep never followed the shepherd out of the pen they would eventually wither and die. Are you connecting the dots? If you cannot hear and follow Jesus' voice, you will wither and die of spiritual thirst and starvation.

Spiritual sensitivity and faith are issues of life and death for us; therefore, it's essential that we learn to recognize God's ways and follow them. But that's the trick, isn't it? God tells us that "my thoughts are not your thoughts, neither are your ways my ways" (Isaiah 55:8).

God's thoughts and actions often defy our logic. God says, "If you want to receive, you need to give. If you want to go up, you've got to go down. If you want to increase, you must decrease. If you want to be exalted, you must be humbled. If you want to live, then you've got to die." This sounds crazy. How do I end up with more if I'm giving everything away? The math doesn't work.

A Need for Reprogramming

Because these teachings are the opposite of the way we naturally think, our gut reaction is to resist. The result is that we stay stuck in the pen. If we want to think God's thoughts, hear His voice, and recognize His ways, we're going to need reprogramming. This is why God needs to take us to the wilderness.

In the wilderness, God reprograms us by turning our world upside down. Things no longer make sense. All the things we relied on—our own understanding, abilities, and strategies—no longer seem to help us. Our fear is that we will wither and die. That's when we reach a crossroad.

At the crossroads, one option is to exit, stage left, and force our way out by clinging to our logical way of doing things. However, the irony in choosing this route is that it takes us back to the sheep pen where our spirit really does wither and die. The second option is to stick it out in the wilderness and let God break our logic and teach us His ways. I was at that crossroad and nearly chose the wrong path.

At the Crossroads

It had been a year since our church had merged and a year since I had a job. With no income and no prospects on the horizon, my loving, supportive wife was, understandably, not calm. One day she got my attention and said, "Dude—get a job!"

You need to understand, I had not spent the year sitting around ignoring our dire straits. I'd been praying for God to show me what to do, but the only answer I sensed from Him was, "Trust me."

I said, "God, we don't have any money. I need a job." And He just said, "Trust me."

In fact, I felt that God didn't even *want* me to get a job, but that didn't make any sense. When I tried to explain this to Charlene, it made even less sense.

Her response was, "How is God honored by our going bankrupt? How is it a good testimony if our house goes into foreclosure?" I had to admit, she was making more sense than I was.

That's when I almost went the wrong way.

I had a friend who was always hiring people. I knew I could get a job with him instantly. All I had to do was ask. So that very day I called him up and said, "I could really use a job right now. Would you hire me?"

His response surprised me. My friend always calls me "Sherwood," but on this day, for whatever reason, he called me "Bishop." He said, "Bishop, did God tell you to call me?"

What kind of job interview question is that? I thought. *Why would he ask me that?* It was a crossroads moment. All I had to do was say, "Yes, God told me to call you," and I'd be hired. But out loud, I admitted, "No, God didn't tell me to call you, but man, I need a job."

My friend paused and said, "Okay, I'll pray. And if the Lord tells me to hire you, I'll call you back." I was stunned. This friend could have hired me in a heartbeat, but he didn't.

But I didn't give up. I had another good friend who had told me how he needed someone he could trust to run things while he was away. So I picked up the phone again and gave him a call.

I said, "I'm your guy. You know me. You know you can trust me and I need a job. Hire me and you'll be able to get some time off." It all made sense. In my mind it was a slam dunk.

Once again, I was blown away by the response. Although he had never met the friend I had just called, he used the exact same words. "Bishop"—which he never calls me—"did God tell you to call me?"

What? I thought. *This is crazy! What does it matter? I need a job now!*

Once again, I knew that if I said, "yes," I'd have a job. It was tempting to say yes, but I admitted that God had not told me to call. My friend showed more wisdom than I. He said, "Man, you're on a journey with God right now. If I hire you and you're not supposed to be here, you're going to mess up *my* stuff. But I'll pray. And if God tells me to hire you, I'll call you back."

Neither friend ever called back.

Within only a few minutes, God spoke the exact same message to me through two different friends who didn't even know each other. God used them to confirm what I'd been sensing—He didn't want me to get a job. He wanted me to stay in the wilderness and wait for Him to provide.

From a logical standpoint, not getting a job was ludicrous. You just don't do things like this. Common sense says to go out and earn a living. And I could have. All I had to do was exit, stage left by telling a small lie. Or I could defy logic and allow God to take me on a faith journey. I chose to defy logic, but I had no idea how I was going to make it without a job.

Asking God

The Bible says, "If any of you lacks wisdom, he should ask God" (James 1:5). Well, I was a guy who lacked wisdom, so I started praying like crazy. "Okay God," I prayed, "how am I going to provide for my family?"

Soon after that, a string of events began to quickly unfold. First, God reminded me of some unused video equipment sitting in my garage that I had forgotten all about. Then He brought a media company across my path that wanted to purchase the equipment.

With very little effort on my part, God provided for my family. By being obedient and seeking His guidance, God had shown me the way.

I now believe that God orchestrated that entire wilderness event to strengthen my faith and heighten my sensitivity to His voice. God had intentionally put me at a crossroad where I had to act before He would act. After I chose to listen and follow, God stepped in and provided for us in an unexpectedly easy way. As a result of this experience, my ability to recognize God's voice grew and so did my faith.

It Takes Repetition

Every athlete knows that building strength and developing skills takes repetition. In the same way, every believer should know that it will take more than one experience to develop the skill of hearing from God, and it will also take more than one experience to build the faith needed to act on what is heard.

In the wilderness, God will repeatedly put us in situations that don't make sense. He will put us in places where we can no longer rely on ourselves, our skills, or our resources. God does this so that we will start listening for His voice and pay closer attention to what we are sensing.

If we take a risk and act on what we hear, God will show up. He will confirm our decisions. That's when we learn in a deeper way what the Spirit's leading feels like in our life; as a result, our trust in God will grow.

During my time in the wilderness, God took me to the crossroads over and over again. Through these experiences I learned to differentiate between logic and God's voice. I learned to recognize God's ways and not just His acts. I learned to be on the front side of what God was doing, rather than being a "forensic Christian" on the back side. In the wilderness, God was transforming me into the man He needed for His next assignment.

Making a "God Call"

By nature, I'm a numbers guy. I like to say, "In God we trust—all others must bring data." Before I make a decision, I want to see the spread sheets and crunch the numbers so I can say, "Yeah, that's a good call." But the truth is I don't need to know if it's a good call. I need to know if it's a *God call*.

I don't need to know if it's a good call. I need to know if it's a God call.

Because of my time in the wilderness I can say with more confidence and frequency, "This is the way God is going." I still plan, check data, and make strategies—but I hold it all loosely. I don't act until I hear from God. If what I hear from God goes against the data and the plans, I'll go with God.

Don't Run

When God told Moses to go to Pharaoh and simply say, "Let my people go"—it made no sense. When the people were trapped against the Red Sea with the Egyptian army closing in on them and God told Moses to respond by raising his arms—it made no sense. When God told Moses to take a million people across a desert to a land they knew nothing about—it made no sense. A logical person would exit, stage left. But a person who knows God's ways will act when God leads.

Before God can use you for a new work, you'll need to be able to hear His voice and have the faith to act on it—even when it makes no sense. So when you find yourself facing situations that make no sense, there's a great chance that God is at work. He is taking you to the crossroads to strengthen your sensitivity and your faith.

When you face those experiences, don't run from them—embrace them. Make the most of them. You will get to know God in the wilderness and learn to recognize His ways. You'll be able to say, "God *is* here," instead of "God *was* there." You'll be on the front side of what God is doing, not the back side. You'll be able to do more than make the "good call," you'll be able to make the "God call."

Chapter Eight

Ground Into Powder

"Whoever falls on this stone will be broken:

but on whomever it falls, it will grind him to powder."

Matthew 21:44 (NKJV).

"I think God is getting ready to take me home."

I vividly remember the moment I said those words. I was at an IHOP, sitting across a table from a good friend, unloading all of my burdens. My friend just listened as I went on. "God has taken away everything," I said. "He's not allowing me to pastor. He's not allowing me to preach. I'm completely broke and behind on my mortgage. I think God may be through with me. Maybe He's accomplished His purpose for my life and He'll soon be taking me home."

God's Purpose for the Wilderness

That day at the IHOP, I was closer to understanding what God was doing in my life than I knew. I was ready to allow God to do anything with my life, even take it. I was a broken man. And that's exactly what God wanted me to be—broken.

God was using my wilderness experience to break me of my self-reliance, and it was a really good thing. When we're broken, God, the Master Potter, can mold us to accomplish His purposes. When we're broken, God can fill us with His power. When we're broken, God can take over and begin to work miracles through us.

A Model of Brokenness

Brokenness is a theme that runs throughout the Bible, with Jesus being the greatest example. Before starting His public ministry, Jesus spent forty days in the wilderness without food or shelter. He allowed himself to be broken—to become totally reliant on God the Father. Then, when Jesus left the wilderness, I find it interesting that his first-recorded sermon starts by saying that those who are broken are the ones who are fortunate (Matthew 5:3).

Throughout His ministry, Jesus modeled a lifestyle of brokenness. He frequently pulled away from the crowds and the "success" to pray and be alone with God. He recognized His desperate need to be reliant on the Father.

In the Garden of Gethsemane, Jesus candidly told His Father, "I don't want to do this." He was in so much anguish that He sweat drops of blood. But then, Jesus completely surrendered himself and said, "Yet not my will but yours be done." That's brokenness.

Finally, on the cross Jesus allowed his very body to be broken, but that brokenness didn't lead to defeat. It led to victory—victory for Jesus and for everyone who calls on His name!

Needing to be "The Guy"

Brokenness, however, is not something I was raised to embrace—not in grade school, not in high school, not in college, and not in my ministry. I was taught that I needed to act like I had it "going on." I was taught that I needed to be perfect. I was taught that I needed to be "the guy," or I would never make it. And I bought into that teaching. We all do at times.

But God takes us to the wilderness to strip away all of our props. He allows us to see who we really are—the good, the bad, and the really bad—and be broken by the truth.

That meeting at IHOP was a turning point in my wilderness experience. After that, I began to recognize what God was doing in my life. I realized that God had work to do in me before I was ready to do His work.

Brokenness as a Way of Life

You may wonder why wilderness times have to last so long. It's because our lifestyle of self-reliance is deeply rooted. It's been developed over a lifetime. It will take time to break free of that old lifestyle and replace it with a new lifestyle—a lifestyle of brokenness. You see, brokenness cannot be a one-time event. It needs to be a way of life. This is what the Bible proclaims.

> *David proclaims*, "You do not delight in sacrifice, or I would bring it; you do not take pleasure in burnt offerings. The sacrifices of God are a broken spirit; a broken and contrite heart, O God, you will not despise" (Psalm 51:16-17).

God proclaims, "I live in a high and holy place, but also with him who is contrite and lowly in spirit, to revive the spirit of the lowly and to revive the heart of the contrite" (Isaiah 57:15).

Jesus proclaims, "God blesses those who realize their need for Him, for the Kingdom of God is given to them" (Matthew 5:3, NLT).

The Apostle Peter proclaims, "Humble yourselves, therefore, under God's mighty hand, that He may lift you up in due time" (1 Peter 5:6).

If you read the Bible, you can't miss the point! You are meant to live a life of brokenness—a life of complete reliance on God. But it takes time. I speak from experience.

Taking Out the Trash

I was a year into my wilderness. Occasionally, I would have the opportunity to preach here and there, but financially, we were barely making it week to week. During this time, a media company offered to put some of my messages on CD so that I could sell them and make a few extra dollars. Sadly, that's all it took for me to start getting full of myself again.

This "full-of-myself" attitude came to a head one afternoon. And the hammer of truth was my wife.

It's comical when I look back at it now. Here I was, barely getting by, but I was imagining myself as a big-time national speaker with my own series of messages for sale. This "full-of-myself" attitude came to a head one afternoon. And the hammer of truth was my wife.

Charlene came home one afternoon to find me sitting in my favorite chair, watching TV, and just chillin' as king of my castle. She walked into the room and could smell the garbage in the kitchen. Women must have an extra sense for that because I hadn't noticed. My wife looked at me—all comfortable in my chair. Then she looked at the garbage. Then she looked at me, took a sniff of the garbage, and said, "Could you please take out the garbage? It stinks!"

That's when words came out of me that stun me to this day. I said, "Don't you know who I am? I am Bishop S. C. Carthen!" I kid you not, I really said that—and I'm embarrassed by it. As soon as the words were out of my mouth, I saw the whites of Charlene's eyes. She put her hands on her hips and snapped, "I don't care who you are, mister. GET UP AND TAKE OUT THE TRASH!"

I don't remember now if I was serious when I said those words or if I was just joking around. But even in humor there is often some truth. Here I was, a year into the wilderness, and I was still trying to fake the funk. I was still full of myself. God had more work to do.

As I walked outside with the garbage, I sensed the Spirit of God say, "Without me, you're nothing more than what's in that trashcan you're carrying." I knew He was right. To this day, taking out the trash has new meaning in my life. But now I try to not let it pile up – not in the house or in my attitude.

The Cost of Leadership

A friend came to see me recently. He was an associate pastor of another church, and he had just been laid off—a casualty of budget cutting. Although he had little savings, he told me he didn't sense God calling him to pursue a position at another church. This didn't make sense to him, so he asked for my thoughts. I smiled and said, "Welcome to the wilderness. Prepare to be here awhile. It's only just begun." I don't think he was encouraged by my words.

The truth is no one talks much about the cost of becoming God's kind of leader. To become the kind of man or woman God uses to accomplish His purposes, you have to let God lead you through the wilderness. It's unavoidable. There's no other way to be broken of your ingrained self-reliance. There's no other way to learn total reliance on God.

My intent in writing this book is to be encouraging, but I need to keep it real. There's no sugar-coating the wilderness experience. It's hard. It will test you. It will also change you. There's a cost you must pay, but it's worth it. Your struggles in the wilderness have a purpose. There's great benefit to be gained when you learn to live a life of brokenness.

Is It Worth It?

This may sound strange, but joy is the result of being broken before God. I used to look for joy through success and having "stuff." Honestly, I don't know that I was even happy back then. I was just driven, trying to be more successful for God's sake. But today my joy comes from being broken and knowing that His heart is my heart. My joy comes from having a right relationship with my Savior, knowing that if I have nothing else but Him, it's enough. My joy comes from serving God and leaving the results to Him.

I have more peace now as well. I used to worry a lot. I worried about how people saw me. Did they see me as a success? Did I look like "the guy?" Did I measure up to expectations? I look back now and shake my head in disgust. Although I was supposedly working *for God*, I was worried about *my* success. That's crazy.

Living a broken life has also made me bolder. I'm willing to take bigger steps of faith. I'm willing to risk failure. I'm no longer concerned about what other people will think of me if I fail. After all, what do I have to lose? I'm already broken.

Joy, peace, and faith—these are the things that my four years of struggling in the wilderness gave to me. Now I'm more connected to God, more attuned to His direction, and more available to be used for His purposes. Now my faith and my character are stronger. I live with greater joy, peace and boldness. Decide for yourself: is spending time in the wilderness worth it? It was to me. And if God ever chooses to lead me back to the wilderness, I will go without a struggle.

Being Intentional

In order for brokenness to become a way of life, we need to be intentional. We need to choose to be broken daily. In Matthew 21:44, Jesus says something profound that is seldom preached on. In referring to himself, Jesus says, "Whoever falls on this stone will be broken: but on whomever it falls, it will grind him to powder" (NKJV).

Jesus has given us a choice. We can choose to intentionally fall on Christ and be broken, or we can try to avoid being broken, and end up being ground to powder. Jesus is driving home the point that we must choose to be broken and stay totally reliant on Him.

A Way of Life

During my four years in the wilderness, I slowly learned what it means to make brokenness a way of life. Our natural tendency is to deny and hide our sin because it threatens our attempts to look successful. But when we are intentional about being broken, we'll do the opposite. We'll seek to be aware of our sinfulness. We'll pay attention to the red flags in our lives. Then, we'll throw ourselves on Christ our Rock by confessing our sins immediately so that sin's power can be broken, and God can remove it before it takes root in our life.

This lesson came to a head one day over a familiar issue—trash! I was on the phone with a woman from the trash company because the "sanitation engineers" had picked up my neighbors' trash but not mine. This helpful lady suggested that the problem must somehow have been my fault. I got hot.

"Look lady, my trash can was right where it was supposed to be, when it was supposed to be. NOW GET SOMEONE BACK HERE TO PICK IT UP!" Then I hung up the phone and headed for my pastor's meeting to go be spiritual.

On the way there, the Spirit of God convicted me. He said, "Sherwood, what are you doing arguing with someone about trash? Who do you think you are?" I was immediately humbled. When I got to my meeting I did do something spiritual. I confessed my "I'm-the-guy" attitude to my peers before it could start taking root in my life.

When people can get me agitated over small stuff, it's a red flag that there's probably something deeper I need to deal with. I need to let go of my need to be right, my need to be in control, my need to be a success. When I see the red flag, it's a sign I need to do some confessing and repenting of attitudes and actions. That's what it looks like to have brokenness as a lifestyle.

But there's more to living a life of brokenness than just recognizing and confessing your sin. It also means allowing yourself to be broken by the things that break God's heart. It means lamenting over the pain in the world. It means crying out to God over the lost condition of people's souls and saying, "Here I am, God. Send me!"

I confessed my "I'm-the-guy" attitude to my peers before it could start taking root in my life.

Broke for Good

Brokenness is the way of the Lord. You can choose to fall on Jesus and be broken, or you can wait to be ground to powder. The reason God takes us to the wilderness is to break us and teach us how to stay broken so that we won't be ground to powder.

If you stick it out in the wilderness—and I pray you will—you'll come out a broken man or woman who knows true life, joy, peace, strength and boldness. You'll be living with God's strength and not your own. You'll allow God to do anything He wants with your life. You'll be ready when God calls you for the "Main Event."

Chapter Nine

Promotion Comes From God

For promotion comes neither from the east,
nor from the west, nor from the south. But God is the judge;
he puts down one, and sets up another."
Psalm 75:6-7 (KJV)

Near the beginning of my wilderness season, I received a phone call from Promise Keepers. They were coming to Sacramento to hold one of their national men's conferences at Arco Arena. That year, at every conference, they had a local pastor speak to the thousands of men attending about what God was doing in their city. They wanted to know if I would do the talk for the Sacramento conference.

I felt truly honored to be asked, but also shocked. The names of several pastors I felt were more qualified came immediately to my mind. But they were asking me. I was humbled.

I asked why they'd chosen me, and they said I had been recommended. I couldn't believe it. This was a big deal. I shared the good news with all my family, friends and peers, and they were genuinely excited for me.

A Wilderness of Lies and Accusations

A few days before the event, I met with a Promise Keepers staff person to go over the talk. However, he didn't seem excited to see me. He barely made eye contact when I shook his hand. I could tell something was up. He started going into some polite conversation, but I didn't want to chit chat. I said, "Let's cut to the chase. What's wrong?"

"I'm sorry to inform you, but I can't have you speak on Friday night."

"Wow," I said, "that's disappointing. What happened?"

"The reason I can't have you speak," he explained, "is because I've talked to your peers and they say that you're arrogant and that you've embezzled money from a fund-raising dinner."

I was stunned. I couldn't believe my peers would say such a thing. I began to think about the guys I was in fellowship with—all of them were godly pastors and leaders in the city. None of those guys had ever pulled me aside to tell me I had a problem with arrogance. They never even alluded to it. I couldn't believe any of them would have said these things about me. I wanted to defend myself. But how do you defend yourself against the claim that you're arrogant without sounding arrogant?

And the charge of embezzlement, now that's serious. It was true that I had been part of organizing a fundraising dinner to honor people who had made a difference in our community. However, we ended up cancelling the event because of low ticket sales. We sent all of the money back to the various businesses that had purchased tickets and even took a loss on the event due to the down payment we had made for the venue. I couldn't begin to imagine who thought I had embezzled money.

I explained all this to the staffer. But he simply said, "My sources say otherwise."

I couldn't believe it. I was certain that he was not talking to my peers. My peers knew the truth. They wouldn't have said these things. The staffer assured me, however, that he had indeed been talking to my peers, but he had to keep their names confidential.

In all honesty, I was deeply disappointed. As a preacher, I dreamed about the day when I could speak to a large audience in a large venue, and to have the chance to share God's heart in Sacramento—my community—would have been special.

When I attended Promise Keepers that Friday, the pastor they picked to replace me was the guy I thought they should have picked in the first place. He was one of the most respected pastors in Sacramento. Even though I had been removed because of a false accusation, I couldn't help thinking that in the end, the right person was speaking that night. God was in control.

God is Always in Control

I once saw a parody of a motivational poster. It was a picture of a football player making a bruising tackle. The caption underneath it read, "SUCCESS: Some people dream of success while others try to crush those dreams."

In life, there will be people who, for whatever reason, will try to stop you from getting ahead. They will criticize you, make accusations, question your reputation, and even spread rumors and tell lies in an effort to keep you from getting ahead. There are others who will make every effort to ingratiate themselves with the "powers that be" so that they become the favorites who are given all the breaks and opportunities ahead of you.

When we miss out on opportunities because of slander or politics, our natural tendency is to blame. We say things like, "If this office wasn't so political, I'd have gotten that job." Or, "Their unwarranted criticism kept me from that promotion." Or, "Unfounded accusations cost me my job." On the surface, there may be truth to those statements. But they deny a deeper truth—God is in control.

Speaking to the home crowd at a Promise Keepers event would have been a great opportunity. It's easy to imagine all the doors that would have opened for me. To say that lies had robbed me of my chance to get ahead would be speaking the truth. But it would deny a deeper truth—God was in control. I was not God's guy for that moment, someone else was.

What We Really Believe

God is in control. We hear that all the time. We say it all the time. We even think we believe it. But when we get criticized, accused, or passed up for promotion, our true belief reveals itself. Often, our reaction is to blame, simmer in anger, or seek revenge. We act as if the people who did these things are in control of our lives and opportunities. Our reaction reveals our true belief, or lack of belief, in God's control.

Attempts at self-promotion also expose our mistrust in God's control. What do you do when you're not getting ahead as fast as you want? How do you react when others are getting the praise you deserve? Do you take matters into your own hands? Do you pour on the charm? Do you try to get in good with the powers that be? Do you start to act as if you're the chosen one?

Through your efforts at self-promotion, you may succeed at creating your own opportunities—assuming you can get people to buy into your act. But you're running on your own power, not God's. These are not God's ways, and they don't lead to God's opportunities.

The truth is promotion comes from God. If God is in control, then God will promote us when we're ready and when He needs us. We can keep trying to manipulate our own miracle, but we will end up being out of place. We won't be where God needs us to be.

We can keep trying to manipulate our own miracle, but we will end up being out of place.

A benefit of the wilderness is that it gives us an honest look at how much trust we really have in God's control. If we respond with blame or self-promotion when opportunities don't come our way, our lack of trust in God's control is revealed. This shows that we're not ready for God's promotion.

Having this kind of honest assessment about ourselves is invaluable. We can see where we're really at and do something about it. When we admit the truth about our level of trust in God's control, God can come and help us strengthen that trust.

Preparing for Promotion

Before God will promote us, He must build our faith to the point that we are completely surrendered to His control. This is what

God was doing in me during my wilderness time. God brought me to a point where I was no longer in control of my life. I had no control over my financial security or even my future. Even though I tried to make things happen for myself, I couldn't. God hindered my every attempt at being in control. Finally, I stopped struggling and accepted that He was in control. When I got to that point, I was able to relax and be at peace. And if you can learn to be at peace in the wilderness, you can be at peace anywhere.

I had finally reached the point where I was willing to do whatever God wanted me to do no matter how big or small. This was an important step in preparing me for promotion because God was going to ask me to do a whopper, something I had no interest in doing. But I'll tell that story later.

If Criticism Sends You Over the Edge, Praise Will Kill You

Part of my wilderness experience was dealing with undeserved criticism and unexpected attacks on my character and reputation. I was hurt and confused. I couldn't understand why God would allow this to happen to me. Then a friend gave me a book by Francis Frangipane called *Stronghold of God.* After reading this book, I was able to make sense of the attacks I was experiencing.

In his book, Frangipane shares about a tough season in his ministry where numerous people were coming against him. They were dogging him at every turn, criticizing his every move, blocking him from going forward. Out of this experience, Frangipane realized that God was using the criticism to strengthen him. As a result of this strengthening, future criticism would not be able to control him.

Frangipane also came to the realization that God was baptizing him in criticism in order to inoculate him against praise. He learned that if criticism sends you over the edge, then praise will kill you. Praise has the power to inflate your pride and deflate your faith. It can also be addictive. Your desire for praise can control your decisions to the point that God is no longer in control. So before God promotes us, He will use the wilderness of criticism to prepare us for success and the praise that comes with it.

Frangipane's comments made sense to me. It gave me a better understanding of what was happening and helped me to accept it. My baptism of criticism was painful, but invaluable. Now I am alert for any signs of pride trying to take root in my life. God will use the wilderness of criticism to do the same thing in your life.

God will use the wilderness of criticism to prepare us for success and the praise that comes with it.

Jesus' Example

It's important to remember that before starting His ministry Jesus also had to surrender Himself and wait on God's timing in the wilderness. There were things Jesus needed to prove to Himself, to the Father, and to the devil before He was ready for promotion.

After forty days without food, at a time when Jesus was physically at His weakest, the devil launched his attack. First, the devil tried to get Jesus to take a short-cut out of His suffering by turning stones into bread. Then, the devil tried to get Jesus to take the route of self-promotion by being a show-off. "Throw yourself off the highest point of the Temple and let the angels catch you," he suggested. Finally, the devil tried to entice Jesus with the praises of men by promising to make him the ruler of every kingdom on earth. Even though Jesus' time in the wilderness had weakened Him physically, it had strengthened Him spiritually, and Jesus was able to easily resist the devil's efforts to gain control of His life.

The Bible says that as soon as the devil left, the angels came and ministered to Him. Jesus had proven that no matter how hot, dry, or painful the journey, He would be obedient to God. No matter what kinds of trials or temptations came His way, He wouldn't take a shortcut out of the wilderness or try to manipulate the circumstances. Jesus had established God's control in His life and now He was ready for promotion.

This is the example we need to follow.

Just Forgive Him

Two years after the Promise Keepers event, I was at an end-of-the-year prayer meeting for local pastors. The leader of the prayer meeting urged us not to take the present year's junk into the New Year. So, we each began to pray, asking God to reveal anything in our lives we needed to confess. In the middle of my prayer, I sensed God saying to me, "The guy who lied about you is going to repent. Forgive him."

About two minutes later, there was a hand on my shoulder. A man was weeping saying, "I've done you wrong and I want to ask your forgiveness."

I didn't even want to look up. I simply said, "I forgive you, brother."

He persisted, "No, you don't understand." His crying turned to sobbing and he said, "I lied about you. I've said stuff about you.

I've prevented you from some things. I said things so people wouldn't like you. I've dogged you. I really need your forgiveness."

This was the man who had prevented me from speaking at the Promise Keepers conference. But the Spirit of the Lord told me, "Just forgive him." So I got up out of my chair, put my arms around him and said, "Man, I forgive you."

This too, was part of my preparation for promotion. Not only did I have to accept people's criticism and false accusations, I had to forgive them. I needed to show that I was so surrendered to God's control that I would be obedient even in forgiveness.

Forgiveness will likely be a part of your wilderness experience as well. Forgiving those who have harmed you will not be easy, but it will be necessary because it's a part of surrendering your life to God's control.

Coming Full Circle

I am now part of a church planting movement called the Bayside Family of Churches. In 2005, all of the Bayside Churches came together for one colossal worship celebration. In Sacramento, the only venue large enough to accommodate us was ARCO Arena.

Now in the denomination I grew up in, when all of the churches gathered, it was the Bishop who spoke. So, I assumed that Ray Johnston, the Pastor who launched the Bayside family of churches, would be the one to speak at this gathering. But Ray asked me to be the preacher.

In all honesty, I didn't think I was the one who should do it. I actually argued with Ray and told him he should be the one to speak. But he said, “No, I want you to do it.”

At this point, my lost opportunity to speak at ARCO hadn’t even crossed my mind. That had been years earlier and I had forgotten about it. It was my wife who said, “Look at this! It’s come full circle.”

When she reminded me of this, I was struck by the fact that promotion comes from God and not anybody else. Although I missed the opportunity to preach to 7,000 men at Promise Keepers, I ended up preaching to 10,000+ people at our Celebration Service.

This was not something I sought for myself. I had forgotten all about ARCO. I had put it out of my mind. But in His timing, God made it all happen. I just had to be willing to let God be in control.

Do You Believe It?

My prayer is that when you’re in a wilderness you won’t try to bail out through self-promotion. Instead, take an honest measure of your faith and surrender yourself to God’s control. And please don’t prolong your pain by wasting your energy playing the blame game. Instead of simmering in anger or lashing back, allow God to baptize you in criticism in order to prepare you for promotion.

God is in control. And if God is in control, then no amount of criticism, accusation, or slander will stop Him from accomplishing His purposes for your life. The only question is: do you really believe that’s true?

Chapter Ten

Designed For Victory

"But thanks be to God! He gives us the victory through our Lord Jesus Christ."
1 Corinthians 15:57

In the 1940's, with the development of jet and rocket engines, planes began to attain speeds approaching mach 1, the speed of sound. As planes approached this speed, however, they would begin to shake violently. Pilots always backed off fearing they would lose control or that their aircraft would shake apart. Soon the term "sound barrier" was born and most pilots believed it would be impossible to break through it. But there was one pilot willing to risk it.

On October 14, 1947, with his plane violently shaking as it approached the speed of sound, Chuck Yeager decided not to back off. Instead, he put his plane and life on the line, pushed forward on the throttle and punched through the sound barrier. To his surprise, he discovered that once he passed mach 1, the shaking stopped and things were smooth on the other side.

Shaken Up

Going through the wilderness is like going through the sound barrier. It will shake you up until you realize you're too full of yourself. It will break you free of the "What I Need to Succeed" list that you cling to. These things get in your way. They keep you from experiencing God's miracles. God wants to shake them out of you.

In the wilderness, God will break you, then He'll remake you.

When you're getting shaken up in the wilderness, chances are you'll want to back off. You'll want some relief. You'll want the struggles to end.

But when you're at the end of your rope, that's the beginning of God's hope. When you've reached a point where you are desperate for God, you're ready to let Him take full control. But if you take a short-cut out of the wilderness, you'll miss out on everything God wants to do in your life.

In the wilderness, God will break you, then He'll remake you. God will take you to the crossroads, so you'll be able to recognize His voice. God will baptize you in criticism, so you'll no longer be swayed by praise. God will take away the things you rely on, so you'll know you can rely on God alone.

Not for the Faint of Heart

These blessings will only become a reality in your life through experience—wilderness experience. This isn't for the faint of heart. But I'm writing to grown folk who are willing to pay the cost—folk who won't back off when life gets shaky.

You may have heard that salvation is free. That's true—Christ paid the penalty for our sins and offers us the free gift of grace. But while salvation is free, following Christ will cost you everything. Jesus said, "If anyone would come after me, he must deny himself and take up his cross and follow me. For whoever wants to save his life will lose it, but whoever loses his life for me will find it" (Matthew 16:24-25).

A cross is where we go to be crucified—to die. That's the price we must pay to experience the miracle of God's power working in us. That's also the price we must pay to experience the miracle of God working through us to transform the world. We must die to ourselves, and let God take over! But we'll never really understand what it means to die to ourselves until we experience it in the wilderness.

There's Victory on the Other Side

"I tell you the truth, unless a kernel of wheat falls to the ground and dies, it remains only a single seed. *But if it dies, it produces many seeds*" (John 12:24). When we die to ourselves, IT'S NOT OVER. Death is not defeat, IT'S VICTORY!

The Apostle Paul, a man whom God took to the wilderness many times, knew from experience that when you push through, there's victory on the other side. Listen to what he has to say:

"I consider everything a loss compared to the surpassing greatness of knowing Christ Jesus my Lord, for whose sake I have lost all things. I consider them rubbish, that I may gain Christ" (Philippians 3:8). In the wilderness, we may lose everything, but we'll gain something far greater: we'll know Christ—

we'll experience His real, living power in our lives. THAT'S VICTORY!

As the Apostle Paul says, "I want to know Christ...and the fellowship of sharing in his sufferings, becoming like him in his death, and so, somehow, to attain to the resurrection from the dead" (Philippians 3:10-11). After death it's not over. There's resurrection. In the wilderness, God will break us and then remake us. THAT'S VICTORY!

Designed for Spiritual Victory

Brothers and sisters, I want you to know that you are designed for victory! But I'm not talking about a worldly victory. I'm talking about a spiritual one. In the world, you'll only have victory when there's no more conflict, no more trouble, or when the game is over and you've come out on top. But in the wilderness there is conflict, there are challenges, and you're not on top. In the wilderness, there's no worldly victory, but there's something better—spiritual victory.

A spiritual victory is greater than a worldly victory. A spiritual victory says, "For Christ's sake, I delight in weaknesses, in insults, in hardships, in persecutions, in difficulties. *For when I am weak, then I am strong*" (2 Corinthians 2:10). A spiritual victory says that in spite of our struggles, "Who shall separate us from the love of Christ? Shall trouble or hardship or persecution or famine or nakedness or danger or sword? No, in all these things *we are more than conquerors* through him who loved us" (Romans 8:35 & 37). A spiritual victory says, "*I can do everything* through (Christ) who gives me strength" (Philippians 4:13).

A spiritual victory doesn't rely on circumstances—it comes in spite of circumstances. The world can be violently shaking us, but we will not back off. We have the strength of Christ in us. We can push through to find out that it's smooth on the other side. Because we have surrendered control over our lives, we can experience God's peace that surpasses understanding.

Your Foundation When Life is Shakin'

The wilderness is a set-up! God orchestrates it all so that we can experience His victory. And once we've experienced God's victory, it will become our foundation when life is shakin'. Now you know you can face anything. You know you can take a lickin' and keep on tickin'. You know that you are more than a conqueror, and you can do anything through Christ Jesus your Lord!

I'm not preaching platitudes here. I know what I'm talking about. I have experienced God's victory even through the worst of circumstances.

As a child—I was repeatedly molested. From the world's point of view, that was a loss. My life today, like so many others, could have been devastated because of those experiences, but God has given me spiritual victory! I am not trapped by my past. God brought me out of that experience without losing my mind and without inflicting the same kind of abuse on somebody else. Today, because I've been there, I have a greater sensitivity towards people who have been wounded or hurt and can offer them the healing presence of Christ. Physically speaking, I lost out as a child—but God has given me victory.

As a teenager—I was drawn into pornography. Like so many

who have been molested, my abuse induced an unhealthy curiosity about sex. In the flesh, I lost, because I didn't look at women or relationships the right way. But God has given me victory. I'm not saying I'm not tempted. I'm saying that thanks to the power of God's Spirit in me, I don't take the bait. I don't even stop to look at it. Today, I'm able to minister to guys entangled by porn and tell them from experience that if they want to be delivered, God will deliver them. Physically speaking, I lost out as a teenager—but God has given me victory.

As a young man—my first marriage dissolved. It's a long story, but I'll cut to the chase. I accept the blame. Even though God used a set of circumstances to clearly tell me not to get married, I didn't listen and went ahead anyway. I failed God and I failed as a husband. I made a mess, but I still expected God to bless. Humanly speaking, I lost. But I humbled myself before God, and in His timing God gave me a second chance. I now have a wife and family that are second to none. They make my life richer. God has given me victory.

As an adult—I have experienced the painful separation of death. I've lost my mother, my father and three of my four siblings. Each time, humanly speaking, I lost. But each time, spiritually speaking, God gave me victory. My sister died at the age of 28. As a family, we were devastated by the loss. I was to preach at her funeral, and I didn't know how I was going to do it. My grief was so strong that I had no strength, no words. But as I started to give the message, I felt God's power take over. It was tangible. I felt it, but I can't describe it. I can't forget it either.

It's become part of my foundation when my world is shakin'. Physically, I lost—but God gave me victory.

Worth The Cost

Is the wilderness tough? Yes! Is the wilderness a place of absolute surrender? Yes! Will the wilderness challenge everything you've ever thought? Yes!

It's true—the wilderness is not for children, but for grown folk, ready to eat solid food. It's true—the wilderness is a place of dying so that Christ can start living through you. It's also true that the wilderness is worth absolutely any cost. That's because there's more to the wilderness than what it costs. There is also victory!

Don't Mistake My Meaning

I need to stop and clarify something. If you think I'm suggesting that it's okay to sin because God will still give you victory, you mistake my meaning. Let me be clear. When we sin, we lose a battle, and we pay a price. For some of you, your wilderness has been of your own making. There are consequences to our sins.

Even though God gave me victory after my divorce, that does not mean I didn't suffer consequences. I had to go through the pain of failure. I had to live with the knowledge that I had deeply hurt my ex-wife. I had to face the damage to my soul caused by disobedience. Even today, there are people I cannot minister to because they feel my divorce disqualifies me from speaking into their lives.

Your sin does not keep you out of God's reach, but it has consequences. Jonah is a perfect example. Jonah knew what God wanted, but he refused to do it. In the end, God came and found him. God gave him victory, but not before Jonah spent time trapped with all the trash and other garbage in the guts of a whale. Keep that in mind the next time you're tempted to go ahead and sin, thinking that God will forgive and give you victory later.

Our God is the God of second chances. If you mess up, life is not over. If you humble yourself and say, "I was wrong and I want to do it right," God will forgive you and give you victory.

But it's always easier to follow Him the first time He calls. So I encourage you to avoid the pain of stupid choices and simply keep close to God through the wilderness. God wants us to live as grown folks who know that His ways are always better than our ways.

A Dream Come True

For a long time, I didn't know if my own wilderness would ever end. I finally came to terms with the fact that God had me in the wilderness for a purpose. He was doing things in my life. He was building my character and strengthening my faith. But I didn't know how long it would take.

I had to embrace the wilderness and allow God to work. Even though my life was being shaken up, I chose to stay in the wilderness with God. It took four long years before God brought me out of the wilderness, but when I got out, I found it was smooth on the other side. God had been preparing me for something special.

In 2002, God gave me a hint of what He was planning, although I didn't understand it. I had a vivid dream in which I was traveling across the country. I was going into various airports looking for "the Boss." I was on a mission—I had to find "the Boss."

Most dreams are usually forgotten the moment you wake up, but not this one. It was burned in my mind. I woke up my wife and told her all about the dream. Her response was, "You woke me up to tell me you were dreaming about Bruce Springsteen?" I decided to let it go.

Two years later, God allowed my path to cross with Ray Johnston, the pastor of Bayside Church in Granite Bay, California, one of the largest and most influential churches in our region. I had invited Ray to be the speaker for a city-wide Martin Luther King Day worship celebration. Out of that connection, a deep friendship developed and Ray asked me to come and preach at Bayside.

When my wife and I walked up to the church, we were instantly impressed. It wasn't the facilities that impressed us—they were meeting at a High School at the time. It was the atmosphere that caught our attention. People were excited. There was energy.

Bayside had a mostly white crowd, and I wasn't sure how they'd react to this black preacher, but they loved on me. By the third service, they were flashing the word "AMEN" on the big screen behind me as I preached. I felt God at work in that place.

As my wife and I drove home, we talked about how impressed we were with the passionate vision Bayside had for reaching their community for Christ. We dreamed of a church like that in our stomping grounds of South Sacramento. Little did we know how big a vision Bayside had for reaching their region.

A couple months later I was having lunch with Ray. I mentioned how great it would be to have a church like Bayside in

South Sacramento. I said, "If you were to start a church there, I'd make it my church home." Ray gave me a funny look and then we went on to talk about important things like how the Sacramento Kings were doing.

It was only a short time later that Ray asked if we could get together. When we met, he shared with me his vision for starting a family of churches throughout the Sacramento region and beyond. He explained that "One of the places we've targeted for starting a church is South Sacramento."

I was excited to hear that. I told him I'd be a member from day one. That's when Ray dropped the bombshell: "We don't want you to be a member," he said. "We want you to be the pastor."

Whoa, I wasn't ready for that. But as we continued to talk and dream about what this church could be, the more excited we became.

I went home that day and told Charlene the news. I said, "The church is going to be called Bayside of South Sacramento, but we're going to give it a little hip-hop feel and call it BOSS for short. What do you think?"

Charlene's eyes just about popped out. She said, "Don't you remember your dream? This is the BOSS you were looking for!" Then my eyes popped out. It had been two years. I had completely forgotten the dream. I was blown away. This church literally was a dream come true.

A Sneak Peek of Heaven

But BOSS is a dream in more ways than one. For years it's been my dream to see more churches become multi-ethnic and better represent what heaven will be like. So when we started BOSS, we launched it to be an intentionally multi-ethnic church. Our staff is multi-ethnic. All of our ministry teams are required to be multi-ethnic. Our worship is multi-ethnic. We sing songs in several different styles and even in different languages. BOSS looks and sounds a little bit like heaven to me!

Maybe you're wondering if this kind of multi-ethnic strategy works. Decide for yourself. Our urban church has been running for four years now. There are approximately 2,500 people who attend on any given weekend. But what's more exciting are the kinds of people God is bringing. Our church is roughly 35% African-American, 35% Caucasian, 20% Latino, and 10% Asian. Even more exciting, we've baptized hundreds of new believers. This truly is a dream come true.

It Was All a Set-up

When I first entered the wilderness, God impressed upon me four things that would happen in my life. God later reinforced that word when a saintly woman (who had no idea of what God had said to me) told me that God had spoken the exact same four things to her as well. God promised that:

1) I would pastor again.
2) It would be to the masses.
3) It would be in a multi-cultural context.
4) It would be with a non-traditional partner.

It had all come true. God had set this all up. This is what the four years in the wilderness had prepared me for.

If the invitation to plant a church had been made a few years earlier, I would have turned it down because I had no interest in being a church planter. But now I was able to let God be in control. Further, a few years earlier, if I had been pastoring a church that grew so quickly, pride might have torn me apart. And If I hadn't let go of my "What I Need to Succeed" list, I'd still be clinging to my cherished gospel music. I'd have quenched the worship we now enjoy that allows people from so many backgrounds to feel welcome. Finally, if I had not learned to let go of control, I'd be having a nervous breakdown sweating the myriad of details involved in running a growing church.

The wilderness was wilder, more difficult, and more unpredictable than I could ever imagined...but if I had to do it all over again, I would do it in a heartbeat.

Amen, All by Myself

The wilderness was wilder, more difficult, and more unpredictable than I could ever have imagined. Throughout this book, I've shared from my heart about the challenges and the pain that I experienced there, but if I had to do it all over again, I would do it in a heartbeat. I wouldn't trade the life I now have with Christ for anything.

God has a purpose for the wildernesses in your life. And because God is with you, He will give you victory no matter how devastating or how dark your wilderness may be. The ride through the wilderness may shake you violently, but once you make it through, it's smooth on the other side. You'll have more peace, joy, confidence, and boldness. You'll have more of Christ's character built into you.

Once you make it through the wilderness, you'll have experienced God in a way that you can't get from a seminar, a CD, a sermon or even this book. You will know God in a way that is real, powerful and first-hand. You'll know God from experience—wilderness experience.

Now you are ready to do whatever God calls you to do, whether or not it makes you look successful. Now you are clay, ready for the Potter to mold, ready for God to use, ready for God's victory.

There aren't many people who get excited about the wilderness. There are even fewer people who want to embrace it. But if the wilderness can do all these things in your life, hopefully you'll join me in saying, "Amen!"

About the Author

Sherwood Carthen is the senior pastor of Bayside of South Sacramento, CA – a rapidly growing, multi-ethnic congregation. He also serves as an NBA Chaplain for the Sacramento Kings. As a gifted preacher, known for his ability to challenge people to a stronger faith, Sherwood receives numerous requests to speak at conferences and churches across the country.

Sherwood is also actively involved in the Sacramento community as the Founder and Director of Our Family Community Foundation which specializes in issues of wellness, wholeness, and faith. Nationally, Sherwood serves on the Board of the National African-American Tobacco Education Network and as President of the National Black Clergy for Substance Abuse Prevention.

About the Author